Cupcakes!

30+ Yummy Projects to Sew, Quilt, Knit & Bake

Edited by Lynn Koolish

C&T PUBLISHING

Text and Artwork copyright © 2009 by C&T Publishing, Inc.

Publisher: **Amy Marson**

Creative Director: **Gailen Runge**

Editor: **Lynn Koolish**

Technical Editor: **Teresa Stroin**

Copyeditor/Proofreader: **Wordfirm Inc.**

Cover/Book Designer: **Kristen Yenche**

Production Coordinator: **Casey Dukes**

Illustrator: **Richard Sheppard**

Photography by **Christina Carty-Francis and Diane Pedersen** of C&T Publishing, Inc., unless otherwise noted.

Published by C&T Publishing, Inc., P.O. Box 1456, Lafayette, CA 94549

Library of Congress Cataloging-in-Publication Data

Cupcakes! : 30+ yummy projects to sew, quilt, knit & bake / edited by Lynn Koolish.

   p. cm.

Summary: "A bounty of cupcakes to make and share, including recipes and decorating ideas. If you quilt, sew, knit, needle felt, craft, or just eat, there's sure to be a cupcake for you"—Provided by publisher.

   ISBN 978-1-57120-796-8 (paper trade : alk. paper)

1. Needlework. 2. Cupcakes. 3. Cake in art. I. Koolish, Lynn. II. Title.

TT715.C87 2009

746.4--dc22

                                        2008050940

Printed in China

10 9 8 7 6 5 4 3 2

introduction

Who doesn't love cupcakes? Perfectly portioned, a cake in miniature, just for one. Plain or fancy, homemade or store bought, cupcakes delight us. For some they are just a delectable snack, for others, they are a happy reminder of birthday parties and good times.

We've whipped up a bounty of cupcakes for you to make and share. And we've even included some of our favorite recipes and decorating ideas.

If you quilt, sew, knit, needle felt, craft, or just eat, there's sure to be a cupcake for you.

contents

THE CUPCAKES **6**

PROJECT INSTRUCTIONS

Zero-Calorie Fabric Cupcakes **31**

A Trio of Felted Cupcakes **33**

Ruffled Cupcake **38**

Knit One Purl Too Cupcakes **40**

Mini Pincushions **42**

Chocolate Cupcake Pincushion **44**

Eat Dessert First Postcard **45**

Cupcakes! A Mini Quilt **46**

The Definitive History of a Cupcake **48**

Save One for Me Quilt **50**

It's a Cupcake Party Invitation **52**

It's Always Time for Cupcakes Clock **53**

Sweet Treats Framed Cupcake **54**

Petal Pot Cupcake Carrier **55**

Sweets & Treats Recipe Box **56**

Sarah's Cuppy Cake Pillow **58**

Cupcake Pajama Party Tote Bag **60**

Robo-Cupcake and Friends **62**

Cutie Cupcake Ponytail Holder **63**

Cupcake Magic Wands **64**

Ode to Cupcakes Shrine **66**

Sweet Strawberry Cupcake Purses **68**

Tiny Treasure Cupcake Pins **71**

Charming Cupcake Bracelet **72**

More than Just a Cupcake Book **74**

Delightful Cupcake Book Cover **76**

Cupcake Lacing Toy **79**

My Little Cupcake Card **80**

Use-for-Anything Cupcake Embellishments ... **82**

RECIPES AND DECORATING IDEAS **83**

TEMPLATE PATTERNS **99**

CONTRIBUTORS **126**

the cupcakes

Wondering what you can do with those remaining scraps of a treasured fabric? Make cupcakes! Whether you make them from cotton or felt, these treats are always low calorie. *Go scrap-happy* and mix-and-match a batch of colorful cupcakes.

For project instructions see pages 31–32 and 38–39.

What could be cozier than felted cupcakes?

Make them for a special occasion or for no occasion at all. It's
so easy to decorate your favorite flavor of cupcake with felt,
yarn, and other trims. Great as pincushions, this trio of felted
treats will get you started, and then you can have fun coming
up with your own designs.

☀ *For project instructions see pages 33–37.*

If you're a knitter, you surely have those odds and ends of leftover yarn from scarves, socks, sweaters, and all the other things you knit. It doesn't take much yarn to knit up a bright and colorful cupcake. Pick pairs of your favorite yarns, and knit a bunch. *Large or small, they're a real treat.*

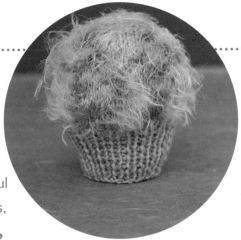

For project instructions see pages 40–41.

Quick to make and fun to give, these minis can be little pincushions or simply a decorative touch. Their petite size just makes them all the more delightful.

For project instructions see pages 42–44.

With perfect little bites of embellishments to *add a bit of whimsy and sparkle*, these are fun projects for little ones to lend a helping hand.

For project instructions see pages 63, 71–73, and 82.

These cupcakes, large and small, give you plenty of opportunity to *put your little scraps to tasty use.* With fusible appliqué, they're fast and easy to make.

For project instructions see pages 46–47.

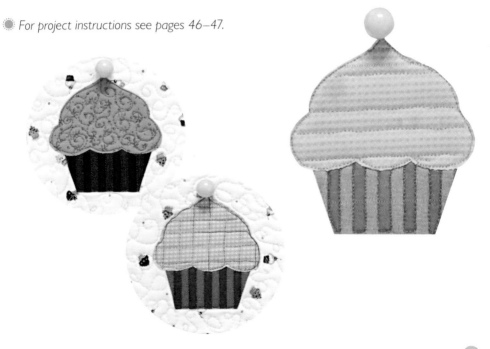

We love cupcakes! Use them to decorate your walls or your table. What could be more fun?

For project instructions see pages 48–49, 62, 64–65 and 66–67.

Need a cheery quilt to *brighten a corner* of your kitchen? Measure the possibilities of this quilted wall-hanging. Fusible appliqué and an easy edging instead of binding make quick work of this tasty treat.

☀ *For project instructions see pages 50–51.*

It's always time for cupcakes! Whether you're looking for recipes, checking the clock, or carrying a special cupcake to a special friend, a cupcake is always a sweet treat.

For project instructions see pages 53–57.

What could be more perfect for sleepovers than a treasured pillow and a cupcake tote bag for jammies and a few necessities?

For project instructions see pages 58–61.

You're invited!
To a cupcake party!
Saturday, August 22 at 2pm
Sally & Jeff's House
7766 Main Street

LIFE IS TOO SHORT

EAT
DESSERT
FIRST

Did you ever realize there were *so many ways to use cupcakes?* From purses to postcards, invitations to book covers, cupcakes are a marvelous motif.

For project instructions see pages 45, 52, 68–70, and 76–79.

Get literary. Use the pages of this versatile book to store your secret thoughts, or make a card to send sweet thoughts to your special little cupcake.

For project instructions see pages 74–75 and 80–81.

project
instructions

Zero-Calorie Fabric Cupcakes

MADE BY: Lynn Koolish
FINISHED SIZE: 3½″ × 3½″ × 3½″

Ingredients

Cupcake top fabric: 5 pieces (pattern on page 99)

Cupcake bottom fabric: 1 strip 2½″ × 17″

Polyester fiberfill

Small yogurt or similar plastic container

Masking tape

Embellishments

Instructions

Note: Seam allowances are ¼″.

CUPCAKE TOP

1. After cutting the pieces for the cupcake top (pattern is on page 99), mark the seam allowance with a dot on the top point and bottom corners of each piece of cupcake top fabric. Clip the inner curve on each piece.

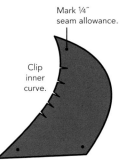

Mark ¼″ seam allowance.

Clip inner curve.

Mark seam allowance, and clip inner curve.

2. Sew the inner curve of 1 piece to the outer curve of a second piece from cut edge to cut edge, matching the dots.

tip: Always sew with the clipped curve up so that you can easily spread the clipped seam allowance as you sew. Pin as often as necessary to prevent the pieces from moving as you sew.

3. Add the remaining pieces in the same fashion, except do not sew all the way to the cut edge at the top. Stop at the dot that marks the ¼″ seam allowance.

4. Sew the last piece to the first piece.

5. Sew a gathering stitch around the bottom edge of the cupcake top.

CUPCAKE BOTTOM

1. Cut the plastic container so it's 1½″ tall.

2. Sew together the short ends of the bottom fabric strip to form a loop.

3. Sew a gathering stitch on both sides of the loop. Gather evenly to fit around the plastic container. Tie off the gathering threads.

Gather evenly around container.

4. Fold about ½″ of the fabric to the bottom of the plastic container, and tape in place.

5. Fold the excess fabric at the top over the top edge of the container, and tape inside.

PUT TOGETHER THE CUPCAKE

1. Stuff the cupcake top with the polyester fiberfill.

2. Gather the cupcake top so that it fits into the cupcake bottom. Tie off the gathering threads.

3. Hand sew the cupcake top to the bottom.

4. Embellish as desired.

A Trio of Felted Cupcakes

MADE BY: Lisa Fulmer Bruce
FINISHED SIZE: 4″ × 4″ × 4″

Ingredients for all Felted Cupcakes

12″ wood skewer

4″-diameter Nerf ball or 6″-long Nerf football

Needle-felting brush and 5-needle punch

Single needle-felting needle

Craft knife such as X-ACTO

Sharp, serrated bread knife

Craft glue

For Birthday Cupcake

Silver glitter glue

Needle and white thread or embroidery floss

White and silver metallic nylon yarn

Multicolored gradient yarn

Straight pins with assorted colors of large bead heads

Purple seed and trumpet beads

Large round bead (skewer needs to fit through)

Wool felt scraps:

> *White: 1 strip 9″ × 2½″ and 1 circle 2″*

> *Purple: 6 hearts (pattern on page 100)*

Wool roving: lavender, red, and blue

For Valentine Cupcake

Pearl-headed straight pins in 2 sizes

Wool roving: brown and red

For Christmas Cupcake

Straight pins with large black bead heads: 9

White and silver metallic nylon yarn

Wool felt:

> *Medium green: 3 holly leaves (pattern on page 100)*

> *Dark green: 6″ × 6″*

> *Red: 9 berries (pattern on page 100)*

Wool roving: dark green and white

Instructions

BIRTHDAY CUPCAKE

1. Use the bread knife to slice the Nerf ball in half. Set aside one half for the top. (If using the football, carve the tip so it's rounded.)

2. Cut the other half down to a flared cylinder for the cupcake base. **Note:** Cut a bit off the rounded end so the cupcake sits flat.

3. Slide the cupcake base and top onto a skewer positioned through the center of each, with the pointed tip coming out the top. Apply glue between the base and the top. Press them together until dry. Leave both ends of the skewer intact to hold the cupcake as you work.

Slide cupcake onto skewer.

4. Wrap the strip of white felt snugly around the base, with the ½″ excess at the bottom. Stitch the felt closed with white thread or embroidery floss, catching some foam with each stitch.

5. Cut 7 notches in the ½″ excess felt at the bottom to create 6 little flaps. Fold each flap to the bottom, overlapping as you go and securing with a few stitches.

6. Snip a small hole in the center of the felt circle for the skewer. Place the felt circle on the bottom of the cupcake to cover the folded flaps. Stitch around the edges to secure.

7. Glue the 6 purple felt hearts upside down, overlapping a bit, all around the cupcake top. Allow the scalloped edges to extend past the edge. Apply glue to only the center area of each heart, not all the way out to the edges. Allow the glue to dry.

8. Needle lavender roving on the top to cover the areas of the Nerf ball that are not covered by felt. Start in the center and gradually work your way to the outer edges, using the side of the needle to guide the roving into the desired place.

9. Needle in a random curvy design all around the top with the multicolored yarn, or mark a shape in advance, then color it in with yarn. Add small pieces of blue and red roving on top of the lavender to make polka dots as desired.

10. Drop a bead onto the pointed tip of the skewer to create a base for the candle. Position the skewer so only 2″–3″ remains at the top. Apply glitter glue to the skewer. Wind metallic yarn tightly around the skewer. Rub a little more glitter glue on the outside with your finger. When dry, trim the excess yarn, and add more glue if needed. Leave about ¼″ of the yarn at the top for a wick.

11. Decorate the cupcake top with the straight pins.

12. To create the flutes of a cupcake paper cup, tie 6 pieces of white and silver yarn into individual 2″ loops by knotting the ends and trimming off the excess. Position the loops evenly around the perimeter of the cupcake base.

Secure loops with straight pins.

Use straight pins to secure each loop at the top and bottom of the cupcake base.

13. Snip off the bottom of the skewer flush with the felt base.

tip: For a finishing touch, ice the edges of the felt hearts with silver glitter glue.

VALENTINE'S CUPCAKE

1. Follow Steps 1–3 of the instructions for the Birthday Cupcake (page 34) to assemble the cupcake onto a skewer.

2. Needle brown roving around the sides and bottom of the base until you get a nice, even surface.

3. Wrap roving under the eave of the cupcake top, and needle it in. Needle roving on the top until you get the desired effect.

4. Lightly dampen your hands with water. Twist and roll a thin strip of red roving tightly between your fingers to form a loose snake of wool. Needle one end into the edge of the cupcake top. Use the side of the needle and your free hand to guide the wool into a scalloped border, and needle into place. Add bits of roving as needed to fill in evenly.

5. To make a fluffy heart decoration, roll a tuft of red roving (larger than the finished size you want for your heart) into a loose ball. Needle the ball of roving through the center into the top of the cupcake a few times to hold it in place. Pull one end down into a soft point for the bottom of the heart, and punch a few times. Continue to use the needle to shape the heart.

Shape heart with needle.

6. Place pearl-headed straight pins in groups of threes—in the center of the heart and along the scalloped border.

7. Trim the skewer from the top and bottom of the cupcake.

CHRISTMAS CUPCAKE

1. Follow Steps 1–3 of the instructions for the Birthday Cupcake (page 34) to assemble the cupcake onto a skewer.

2. Trace 2 concentric circles onto the dark green felt. The inner circle should fit snugly around the top of the cupcake base, and the outer circle should be about ½″ wider. Trim this ring from the felt and slide it up the cupcake base so that it sits flush under the eave of the cupcake top, extending out a bit. Glue it into place against the foam. This will give you a guideline for needle felting the roving so that the final cupcake size is thicker and fluffier than the foam form.

3. Needle white roving around the base and bottom. Needle dark green roving on the top.

4. Apply a strip of glue down the center of each holly leaf, and press into the desired position on top of the cupcake. Glue the berries in clusters of 3 near or on the top of each leaf.

5. Push one black straight pin into each berry, off center.

Add holly leaf and berries.

6. Wrap metallic yarn around the cupcake base (just below the green felt ring) a few times, tie off, and tuck the ends inside.

7. Trim the skewer from the top and bottom of the cupcake.

 tip: These versatile cupcakes can be used as pincushions, as memo holders, or simply as sweet decorations sitting on a dessert plate.

Ruffled Cupcake

MADE BY: Becky Goldsmith
FINISHED SIZE: 3″ × 3¼″ × 3″

Ingredients

Gold wool felt: 1 strip 1¾″ × 7¾″ and 1 circle 2¼″ in diameter

Darkest red wool felt: 1 circle 3¼″ in diameter

Deep red wool felt: 2 circles 2¼″ in diameter

Deep purple wool felt: 2 circles 2¼″ in diameter

Coral wool felt: 2 circles 2¼″ in diameter

Pink wool felt: 1 circle 2¼″ in diameter

Gold embroidery floss to match felt

Darkest red embroidery floss to match felt

Lime green rickrack: 1 piece 7¾″ long

Cardboard: 1 circle 2½″ in diameter

Uncooked rice: ¼ cup

Polyester fiberfill

Instructions

1. Place the rickrack ½″ away from one long edge of the gold wool strip, and stitch in place.

2. Overlap the ends of the gold felt strip ¼″ to make the cupcake base. Stitch them together with matching embroidery floss.

3. Place the gold felt circle in place at the bottom of the cupcake. Stitch it in place.

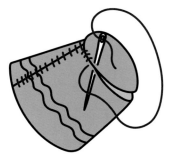

Stitch circle to bottom.

4. Place the cardboard circle inside the bottom of the cupcake. Pour uncooked rice in the bottom of the cupcake to give it some weight. Add stuffing to fill out the cupcake.

5. Fold a coral circle in half and then in half again. Use the darkest red embroidery floss to stitch the folds at the point (so that the circle stays folded). Use the same floss to stitch the pointed end to the center of the large, darkest red felt circle. Knot the thread.

6. Fold the remaining circles, and sew them to the darkest red circle—close to, but not on top of, the first coral circle.

7. Place the ruffled cupcake top on the cupcake base. Stitch the 2 pieces together.

Stitch top to base.

Add folded felt circles.

Knit One Purl Too Cupcakes

MADE BY: Lynn and Ruth Koolish
FINISHED SIZES: 4″ × 5″ × 4″ (regular), 2½″ × 3″ × 2½″ (mini)

Ingredients

2 different yarns of similar weight:
For the regular cupcake, use worsted weights. For the mini cupcake, use fingering weights.

Knitting needles, straight or double-pointed: For the regular cupcake, use size 4 or 5 needles. For the mini cupcake, use size 1 or 2 needles.

Polyester fiberfill

Lightweight cardboard, 4″ × 4″

Scrap of fabric to match cupcake base yarn, 5″ × 5″

Row marker for knitting in the round

Weight such as a washer

Instructions

note: You can use double-pointed needles and knit in the round, or use straight needles and sew the cupcake together after knitting.

1. Cast on 40 stitches. If you are using double-pointed needles, join the stitches, making sure not to twist them. Place a marker at the beginning of the round.

2. Knit ribbing (either knit 2, purl 2; or knit 1, purl 1), 2″ for regular or 1″ for mini cupcakes.

3. Change to the frosting color, and knit 1 make 1 to the end of the row. You should now have 80 stitches.

4. In stockinette (knit 1 row, purl 1 row), knit ¾″ for the regular size or ¼″ for the mini. If you are using double-pointed needles, continue knitting in the round the same amount as for straight needles.

5. Decrease as follows:

Knit 8, knit 2 together repeat to end of row.
Purl 1 row (or knit 1 row if knitting in the round).
Knit 7, knit 2 together repeat to end of row.

Purl 1 row (or knit 1 row if knitting in the round).

Knit 6, knit 2 together repeat to end of row. Purl 1 row (or knit 1 row if knitting in the round).

Knit 5, knit 2 together repeat to end of row. Purl 1 row (or knit 1 row if knitting in the round).

Knit 4, knit 2 together repeat to end of row. Purl 1 row (or knit 1 row if knitting in the round).

Knit 3, knit 2 together repeat to end of row. Purl 1 row (or knit 1 row if knitting in the round).

Knit 2, knit 2 together repeat to end of row. Purl 1 row (or knit 1 row if knitting in the round).

Knit 1, knit 2 together repeat to end of row. Purl 1 row (or knit 1 row if knitting in the round).

Knit 2 together repeat to end of row. Purl 1 row (or knit 1 row if knitting in the round).

6. Knit 2 together until there are only 2 stitches left.

7. For straight needles, bind off; then sew the edges together. For double-pointed needles, break the yarn, leaving a 6″ tail. Thread the tail through the 2 remaining stitches, and hide the tail inside the cupcake.

8. Stuff the cupcake with polyester fiberfill.

9. Cut a circle from light cardboard to use as the base, 2¼″ in diameter for the regular cupcake or 1¼″ for the mini cupcake.

10. Cut a fabric circle that is 1″ larger all around than the cardboard circle (4¼″ for the regular cupcake or 3¼″ for the mini cupcake). Hand stitch ¼″ in from the outside edge of the fabric, and gather the fabric around the cardboard circle. Tie off the thread to secure.

Gather fabric around cardboard circle.

11. Leave the cardboard in the fabric, and sew the bottom of the cupcake in place, slipping in the washer or similar weight.

12. Embellish as desired.

 tip: For a rounder top, skip the plain knit/purl row for the last few rows, and just decrease every row.

Mini **Pincushions**

MADE BY: Kiera Lofgreen
FINISHED SIZE: 2¼″ × 2½″ × 2¼″

Ingredients

Fabric: 2 circles 2″ in diameter,
1 circle 1½″ in diameter, 1 strip
2″ × 7½″

*fast2fuse Double-Sided Fusible
Stiff Interfacing (heavyweight):*
1 circle 1½″ in diameter

Trims for the frosting: white chiffon
ribbon for a light, creamy look;
brightly colored twill tape for an
eye-catching, sugar-overload look;
sheer fringe for a fun, snowball look;
or silk flower heads for a fancy touch

Polyester fiberfill

Instructions

CUPCAKE BOTTOM

1. Matching the raw edges and right sides together,
sew a 2″ fabric circle to one of the long sides of the
fabric strip, using a ¼″ seam allowance. Leave ¼″ free
at the beginning and end of the strip for joining later.
When finished, you should have an open cylinder
of fabric.

Open cylinder of fabric

2. Center the 2 remaining fabric circles, 1 on top of the other, with the circle of fast2fuse in between. Fuse the layers together to create a sandwich. This will be the bottom of your cupcake, because the fast2fuse will give that end a little stability.

3. With the smaller circle of the fabric sandwich facing out (as if it were the wrong side of the fabric), hand baste the right side of the larger circle to the right side of the remaining long edge of the fabric cylinder, with a scant ¼" seam allowance. Again leave ¼" free at the beginning and end of the long edge of the cylinder.

4. Machine stitch with a small stitch length just to the inside of the hand-basting line, with a ¼" seam allowance. Do not catch the fast2fuse in the seam.

5. Turn the cylinder right-side out, and stuff it densely with fiberfill.

6. Hand sew the side opening closed.

DECORATING AND FINISHING

tip: These cupcakes are fun little pincushions, but save the delicate trims for cupcakes that will just be decorative. Chiffon, for example, looks wonderful as a frosting but won't hold up well after repeated pin punctures.

1. Pile, fold, twist, spiral, and sculpt your trims until you get the frosting look you desire.

2. Sew the trim securely to the top of the cupcake with matching thread.

3. For a finishing touch, wrap the cupcake with trim, such as a 1" ribbon or an eyelet lace.

Chocolate Cupcake Pincushion

MADE BY: Casey Dukes
FINISHED SIZE: 2½″ × 3″ × 2½″

Ingredients

Chocolate brown felt: 5″ × 9″

White raw wool: handful

Pink silk ¼″-wide ribbon: 18″

Pink embroidery floss

Fabric adhesive such as Fabri-Tac

Needle-felting tool

Round weight such as a heavy washer

Instructions

1. Fold the strip of brown felt in half, and align the fold with the dotted edge of the cupcake side pattern (page 101). Trim along the solid lines. Also, cut 1 cupcake bottom circle.

2. Align the edge of the bottom circle with the bottom edge of the side piece, and whipstitch about ¹⁄₁₆″ from the edge using 3-strand embroidery thread.

3. After stitching the bottom, tuck the longer end of the side piece inside the cup. Stitch up the side to finish it off.

4. Place the round weight in the bottom of the cup.

5. Stuff the felt cup with white raw wool so that it bulges out quite a bit at the top. Apply a bead of fabric glue around the inside rim of the felt cup, and press gently to secure the raw wool. Use a needle-felting tool to felt the cupcake top, working it into a nice, round shape.

6. Tie the ribbon in a bow around the top of the felt cup. Use for decoration or as a pincushion.

Eat Dessert First **Postcard**

MADE BY: Gladys Love
FINISHED SIZE: 4″ × 6″

Ingredients

Front fabric: 4″ × 6″

Backing fabric: 4″ × 6″

Paper cup fabric: 3″ × 6″

Sparkly fabric scrap for icing

fast2fuse Double-Sided Fusible Stiff Interfacing (heavyweight): 4″ × 6″

Variegated thread

Beads: 2 for candy on top

Instructions

1. Iron the front fabric to the fast2fuse.

2. Embroider or ink the words on the front fabric.

3. Pleat the paper cup fabric by stitching with a twin needle or by pressing and topstitching.

4. Cut the pleated fabric to fit the cupcake cup (pattern on page 109), leaving enough fabric to fold under on both sides and the bottom. Place the cup, with the sides and bottom folded under, on the front of your postcard, and pin in place. Leave the top edge raw. Sew the cup to the postcard.

5. Cut a piece of sparkly fabric for the icing (pattern on page 109), leaving enough fabric to fold back the top rounded edge.

6. Place the icing on top of the cup, and bunch up the edges a little bit to create a slightly raised surface. Stitch down the icing.

7. Satin stitch scallops where the icing meets the paper cup.

8. Scatter zigzag stitches for crumbs.

9. Iron the backing fabric to the back of the postcard.

10. Add the beads at the top of the icing.

11. Use a wide zigzag satin stitch to sew around the outside edges of the postcard.

Cupcakes! A Mini Quilt

MADE BY: Lynn Koolish
FINISHED SIZE: 24″ × 24″
See page 16 for a complete quilt photo.

Ingredients

Block background fabric: 9 squares 6″ × 6″ (½ yard)

Scraps for cupcake appliqués

Border corner blocks: 4 scraps 3″ × 3″

Sashing fabric: 6 strips 1¼″ × 6″, 4 strips 1¼″ × 18½″, and 2 strips 1¼″ × 20″ (¼ yard)

Border fabric: 4 strips 3″ × 20″ for borders, additional strips for binding (¼ yard)

Backing fabric: 26″ × 26″ (¾ yard)

Batting: 26″ × 26″

Decorative trim: 4½ yards (optional)

Buttons

Paper-backed fusible web, 17″ wide: ½ yard

Instructions

Note: Seam allowances are ¼″.

1. Iron paper-backed fusible web to the wrong side of the fabric scraps for the cupcake appliqués. Remove the paper backing.

2. Use the patterns on page 102 to cut out the top and bottom pieces for 9 cupcakes.

3. Reduce the cupcake pattern 50%, and cut out pieces for 4 mini cupcakes for the corner blocks.

4. Create 9 blocks by fusing the cupcake pieces to the block backgrounds.

5. Sew the 1¼″ × 6″ sashing pieces between the blocks to create 3 rows. Press.

6. Sew the rows together with the 1¼″ × 18½″ sashing strips. Press.

7. Sew a 1¼″ × 18½″ strip on each side. Press.

8. Sew the 1¼" × 20" sashing strips on the top and bottom. Press.

9. Sew border strips to the top and bottom. Press.

10. Fuse the mini cupcakes to the corner blocks. Sew the corner blocks to each end of the remaining border strips. Press.

11. Sew the remaining border strips to the sides. Press.

12. Layer the backing, batting, and quilt top. Baste.

13. Quilt and bind. Embellish with trim and buttons.

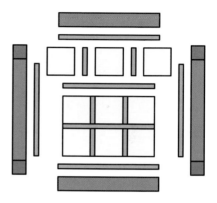

Quilt Assembly Diagram

The Definitive **History of a Cupcake**

MADE BY: Laura Wasilowski
FINISHED SIZE: 5 panels, each 4″ × 4″
See page 18 for a complete photo.

Ingredients

Light blue fabric: 5 rectangles 4″ × 6″
(¼ yard)

Orange fabric: 5 rectangles 2½″ × 6″
(¹/8 yard)

Blue fabric: 12″ × 12″

Light yellow fabric: 8″ × 8″

Green fabric: 8″ × 8″

Red fabric: 2″ × 6″

Pink fabric: 6″ × 6″

Backing fabric: 5 squares 3½″ × 3½″
(¼ yard)

*fast2fuse Double-Sided Fusible Stiff
Interfacing (heavyweight):* 5 squares
4″ × 4″

*Paper-backed fusible web, 17″ wide
(Wonder-Under):* 2 yards

Pinking rotary cutter blade

*Black ultra fine point Sharpie marker
or lead pencil*

Instructions

1. Fuse Wonder-Under to all the fabrics, following the manufacturer's directions. After the fabric cools, remove the paper backing (release paper) in one sheet, and keep for the steps below.

2. Place a fast2fuse square on release paper. Center a light blue rectangle horizontally on top, leaving 1″ extending off the top and side edges of the panel.

3. Center an orange rectangle horizontally overlapping the lower edge of the light blue wall fabric by ½″. Fuse-tack (iron lightly for a few seconds) the fabrics in place.

4. Turn over the panel. Wrap the fabric to the back at the top and bottom, and fuse in place. Fold and wrap the side fabrics onto the back, forming miters at each corner. Fuse-tack in place.

5. Place a backing square on the back. Fuse-tack in place.

6. Place release paper on the egg pattern from the first panel (page 103). Trace with a black Sharpie marker or a lead pencil.

7. Place the ink side of the drawing onto the glue side of the light yellow egg fabric. Fuse-tack in place.

8. After the fabric cools, remove the paper. The ink or lead will have lightly transferred to the glue. Cut out the egg shape from the fabric just inside the line.

9. Repeat Steps 6–8 with the remaining pattern parts for the first panel. Free-cut small elements like the flower, flower center, and string.

10. Place the pattern parts on the front of the first panel, using the pattern as a guide. Note that some pattern parts are stacked onto other elements.

11. Repeat the process for the remaining 4 quilt panels, using the patterns (pages 104–107) as a guide.

12. Steam set the front and back of the quilt panels.

13. Use as separate panels, or join the panels with a zigzag machine stitch.

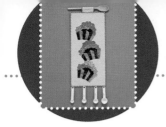

Save One for Me Quilt

MADE BY: Karen Flamme
FINISHED SIZE: 10" × 22" (without hanging loop)

Ingredients

Yellow cotton fabric: 1 rectangle 10" × 22" and 2 squares 4" × 4" (1 fat quarter)

Dark purple cotton fabric: 1 rectangle 4" × 15" (1 fat quarter)

Light purple cotton fabric: 1 rectangle 4" × 15" (1 fat quarter)

Assorted polka dot cotton fabrics: 5 squares 6" × 6" (¼ yard)

Chocolate brown cotton: 1 rectangle 7" × 10" (¼ yard)

Backing fabric: 1 rectangle 10" × 22" (1 fat quarter)

Aqua rickrack, medium-width: $2^{1}/_{8}$ yards

Paper-backed fusible web, 17" wide (Wonder-Under): 1¼ yards

fast2fuse Double-Sided Fusible Stiff Interfacing (regular or heavyweight): 1 rectangle 10" × 22"

Wooden spoon

Measuring spoons

Instructions

1. Fuse Wonder-Under to the back of the light and dark purple, chocolate brown, and polka dot fabric pieces, following the manufacturer's instructions. Remove the paper backing.

2. Cut the following, using the patterns on page 108:

   Light purple fabric: 9 cupcake holders (A)
   Dark purple fabric: 9 cupcake holders (B)
   Brown fabric: 3 cupcakes
   Polka dot fabrics: a total of 9 frostings

3. Beginning with the bottom cupcake, alternately place 3 light (A) and 3 dark (B) purple cupcake holder appliqués in position on the 10″ × 22″ yellow background rectangle.

4. Place the cake appliqué at the top of the cupcake holder pieces, sliding the edge of the cake under the top of the holder. Fuse the pieces in place.

5. Place 3 different color polka dot appliqués in position on top of the cake. Fuse them in place.

6. Repeat Steps 3–5 for the other two cupcakes, tilting them as shown in the photo on page 20.

7. To make the hanging loop, place the 2 yellow 4″ × 4″ squares right sides together, and stitch 2 sides, leaving 2 opposite sides open. Turn right-side out, press, and stitch rickrack on both seamed sides. Fold the loop in half, and position the raw edges in the center of the short side of the fast2fuse. Sew in place.

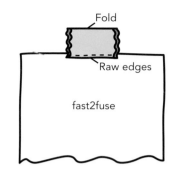

Stitch hanging loop to fast2fuse.

8. Fuse the backing to one side of the fast2fuse (use nonstick cloth to protect ironing board).

9. Fuse the completed front to the other side of the fast2fuse.

10. Quilt if desired.

11. Finish by stitching rickrack around the outside edge.

12. Hand stitch measuring spoons to the bottom edge. Insert the wooden spoon in the top loop, and hang.

It's a Cupcake **Party Invitation**

MADE BY: Mary Link
FINISHED SIZE: 5″ × 5″

Ingredients

Adjust amounts as needed if you enlarge or reduce the patterns. For each invitation you'll need the following:

Fabric: 2 pieces 4″ × 4″ for cupcake base, 2 pieces 3″ × 4″ for cupcake top

Cardstock: 1 piece 3″ × 4″ for invitation information

fast2fuse Double-Sided Fusible Stiff Interfacing (heavyweight): 4″ × 6″

Embellishments of choice (glitter, rickrack, chenille strips, pom-poms)

Glue

Paper punch

Brass fasteners

Permanent fabric pen (optional)

Instructions

1. Use the patterns on page 110, enlarging or reducing as desired.

2. For each invitation, cut 1 whole cupcake shape and 1 cupcake top from fast2fuse. Also, cut 1 cupcake top from cardstock.

3. Iron fabric to the back of the fast2fuse. Trim, using the fast2fuse as a guide. Iron fabric to the front of the fast2fuse. Trim, using the fast2fuse as a guide.

4. Print or write the invitation information on the cupcake top cardstock.

5. Punch holes in the marked spots. Layer the cardstock on top of the whole cupcake and the cupcake top on top of the cardstock, all right sides up. Secure with a brass fastener.

6. Embellish as desired. Make sure to glue the pompom to only the top of the brass fastener so that the cupcake top can spin open.

It's Always Time for **Cupcakes Clock**

MADE BY: Lynn Koolish
FINISHED SIZE: 8″ × 7½″

Ingredients

Cupcake top fabric: 1 piece 8½″ × 6″
Cupcake base fabric: 1 piece 8″ × 4″
Backing fabric: 1 piece 8½″ × 8″

fast2fuse Double-Sided Fusible Stiff Interfacing (heavyweight): 1 piece 8½″ × 8″, 1 piece 8½″ × 6″
Clock kit with movement for ³/₁₆″ surfaces, hands, and numbers
Fabric glue (Fabri-Tac)

Instructions

1. Enlarge a cupcake pattern of your choice (pages 122–124) or use the pattern on page 111, and enlarge it 200%.

2. Cut 1 whole cupcake and 1 cupcake top from the fast2fuse, using the enlarged pattern.

3. Iron the backing fabric to the fast2fuse whole cupcake, and trim to size, using the fast2fuse as a guide.

4. Iron the cupcake top fabric onto the fast2fuse cupcake top, and trim to size, using the fast2fuse as a guide.

5. Place the cupcake base fabric on the base of the whole cupcake so that the cupcake top will cover the top edge, allowing enough fabric to fold over the side and bottom edges. Iron to fuse in place. Fold the excess fabric to the back, and glue in place.

6. Glue the cupcake top in place. Quilt as desired.

7. Use small, sharp scissors to cut a hole just large enough for the stem of the clock movement. Mount the clock movement following the manufacturer's directions.

8. Arrange and glue the numbers around the clock face, and attach the hands.

Sweet Treats **Framed Cupcake**

MADE BY: Joni Pike-Shank
FINISHED SIZE: 6½″ × 6½″

Ingredients

White cotton background fabric:
1 piece 8″ × 8″

Cotton batting: 1 piece 8″ × 8″

Paper-backed fusible web:
1 piece 3″ × 7″

Fabric stabilizer or white tissue paper

Pink print cotton fabric: 2″ × 3″ scrap

Stripe print cotton fabric:
2″ × 3″ scrap

12 small seed beads: 3 each pink,
blue, yellow, and purple

White picture frame with at least a
3⅝″ × 3⅝″ photo opening

Pink rayon thread

Pink or white embroidery floss

White ¾″–wide grosgrain ribbon: 20″

Black ultra-fine point permanent pen

Assorted colors of fabric glitter and adhesive

Masking tape

Instructions

1. Iron the fusible web to the back of the pink and stripe fabric scraps. Remove the paper backing.

2. Using the patterns on page 112, cut the cupcake base from the stripe fabric, and the frosting from the pink fabric.

3. Trace the lettering (page 112) onto the white cotton background fabric with an ultra-fine point pen.

4. Fuse the appliqué pieces to the background fabric.

5. Machine appliqué the raw edges.

6. Embellish with fabric glitter.

7. Layer batting under white cotton background, and use embroidery floss to embellish with beads.

8. Trim to 4″ × 4″, or ½″ larger than the opening in your frame. Baste around the outside edge to stabilize. Insert in the picture frame.

9. Knot the white ribbon around the picture hangers on the back of the frame to make a hanging loop.

Petal Pot Cupcake Carrier

MADE BY: Kerry Graham
FINISHED SIZE: 4½″ × 6½″ × 4½″

Ingredients

3¹/₂″ × 4¹/₂″ Ready-to-Go! Mini Petal Pot (available from craft stores or www.ctpub.com)

3³/₄″-diameter clear plastic ornament ball (available in craft stores)

Vellum: 12″ × 12″ sheet

1″ wooden bead for the cherry

Small stick for the cherry stem

Acrylic paint: berry red, light pink, yellow, pearl lustre medium

Foam paintbrush

Rhinestones

Glue

Instructions

1. Trace Template A (page 113) onto the vellum. Place a template long edge next to a long edge of the tracing. Trace again. Repeat 5 times. Extend the last panel by ¼″ to provide an overlap. Cut out the traced shape.

2. Fold the vellum shape across its width to create ¼″-wide vertical pleats.

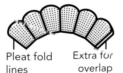

Pleat fold lines   Extra for overlap

Fold pleats into vellum.

3. Trace Template B (page 113) onto the leftover vellum and cut it out. This is the bottom of the cupcake carrier.

CUPCAKE CARRIER

1. Paint the inside and outside of the petal pot. Allow to dry.

2. Stretch the vellum around the pot, and line up each vellum panel with a panel on the pot.

3. Overlap the open short edges of the vellum, and glue together. Glue the vellum to the pot at this edge only and at the bottom.

LID AND CHERRY HANDLE

1. Cut off the hanging loop from half of the ornament ball. Embellish with rhinestones.

2. Paint the 1″ wooden bead berry with the red and then the pearl lustre. Paint the stem with pearl lustre.

3. Glue the stem into the bead, and glue the bead onto the lid.

Sweets & Treats Recipe Box

MADE BY: Lynn Koolish
FINISHED SIZE: 6¾″ × 4¾″ × 3¾″

Ingredients

File card box such as Ready-to-Go! Indie File Box (available from craft stores or www.ctpub.com)

Cupcake fabric: 8¹/2″ × 5¹/2″ for the top, 5″ × 21¹/2″ for the box (¹/4 yard)

Contrasting fabric: 2¹/2″ × 21¹/2″ for the band, 3″ × 5³/4″ for the bottom (¹/4 yard)

Batting: 6³/4″ × 3³/4″ for the top, 3″ × 21″ for the box, 1¹/2″× 21″ for the band

Acrylic paint

Fabric glue

Assorted embellishments (optional)

Instructions

1. Paint the inside of the box and the inner edge.

2. Center the 6¾″ × 3¾″ piece of batting on the wrong side of the 8½″ × 5½″ piece of cupcake fabric, and quilt to add texture.

3. Center the quilted fabric on the top of the box. Glue down the sides, folding the corners.

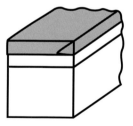

Glue down sides.

4. Sew the short ends of the 5″ × 21½″ piece of cupcake fabric together with a ¼″ seam.

5. Place the 3″ × 21″ piece of batting ½″ down from a long edge on the wrong side of the sewn cupcake fabric from Step 4. Fold the top edge of the fabric over the batting, and topstitch. Turn fabric-side out.

6. Slide the fabric and batting onto the box. Center the seam at the back of the box, and align the topstitched edge with the outside top edge of the box. Glue in place.

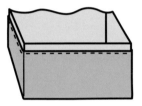

Glue fabric and batting in place.

7. Fold and glue the excess fabric to the bottom of the box. Glue the 3″ × 5¾″ piece of contrasting fabric to the bottom.

8. Sew the short ends of the 2½″ × 21½″ contrasting fabric together with a ¼″ seam.

9. Center the 1½″ × 21″ piece of batting on the sewn band from Step 8, fold both edges of the fabric over the batting, and topstitch. Turn fabric-side out.

10. Slide the contrasting band around the top, covering the raw edges. Glue in place.

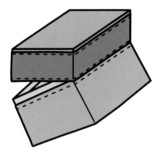

Slide band in place.

11. Embellish as desired.

 tip: Decorate the divider cards by fusing fabric to them and embellishing them with cut-out cupcakes.

Sarah's Cuppy Cake **Pillow**

MADE BY: Fran Demar
FINISHED SIZE: 14" × 14"

Ingredients

White fabric: 1 square 6½" × 6½" for background

Assorted pink fabrics: 4 squares 2" × 2" for corner triangles; 2 strips 2½" × 7½" and 2 strips 2½" × 11½" for sashing (¼ yard)

Black fabric: 2 strips 1" × 6½" and 2 strips 1" × 7½" for sashing; 2 strips 1¾" × 11½" and 2 strips 1¾" × 14" for border (⅛ yard)

Assorted scraps for appliquéd cupcake top (icing), cupcake bottom, and cherry

Pillow back fabric: 2 pieces 10½" × 14" (⅓ yard)

Paper-backed fusible web: 1 piece 8" × 8"

Dark pink and brown embroidery floss

Glitter paint for icing swirls and cherry (optional)

14" × 14" pillow form

Instructions

Note: Seam allowances are ¼".

1. Place the pink 2" × 2" squares on the corners of the white 6½" × 6½" square, and stitch diagonally across the corner squares as shown. Trim and press the triangles open.

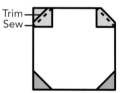

Stitch diagonally across corner squares.

2. Trace the cupcake frosting, cupcake base, and cherry patterns (page 114) onto the paper side of the paper-backed fusible web. Cut out each piece, leaving approximately ¼" around the edge. Fuse to the back of the appropriate fabric, and cut out on the lines.

3. Using the photo on page 25 as your guide, place the pieces on the white 6½" × 6½" square. Place the cupcake base first, then the frosting, then the cherry, overlapping slightly, and fuse.

4. Use 3 strands of dark pink embroidery floss to stem stitch around the appliqué. Add 2 lines of stem stitching to create the cherry stem, using the brown embroidery floss. Or, if you prefer, machine satin stitch around the edges and the stem.

5. Sew the black 1" × 6½" strips to the top and bottom of the center square. Press toward the strips. Sew the black 1" × 7½" strips to the sides of the center square. Press toward the strips.

6. Sew the pink 2½" × 7½" strips to the top and bottom of the pillow. Press toward the pink strips. Sew the pink 2½" × 11½" strips to the sides. Press toward the pink strips.

7. Sew the black 1¾" × 11½" strips to the top and bottom of the center square. Press toward the black strips. Sew the black 1¾" × 14" strips to the sides of

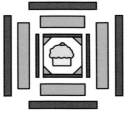

Pillow Assembly Diagram

the center square. Press toward the black strips.

8. Fold over ¼" on a long edge of each 10½" × 14" pillow back piece, and press. Fold over the same edge another 1½" to form a hem, and press. Sew down the folded edge.

9. Place both pillow back pieces on top of the pillow top, right sides together, matching the raw edges and overlapping the finished edges. Sew around the edge.

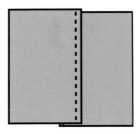

Overlap sewn edges for pillow back.

10. Turn the pillow right-side out.

11. Insert a 14" × 14" pillow form.

tip: To make the cupcake even more delicious, add glitter paint to the frosting and the cherry.

Cupcake Pajama Party **Tote Bag**

MADE BY: Teresa Stroin
FINISHED SIZE: 12″ × 13″ × 12″

Ingredients

White-on-white fabric: 1 rectangle 15″ × 40″ (¹/2 yard)

Striped fabric: 1 rectangle 7¹/2″ × 20″ (¹/4 yard)

Ribbon: approximately 40″

Buttons: 2 large and assorted sizes, as desired

Instructions

Note: Seam allowances are ¼″ unless otherwise noted.

1. Sew a basting stitch with a scant ¼″ seam allowance down one of the long sides of the white fabric.

2. Evenly gather the basting stitch until the edge of the white fabric is 20″ wide.

3. Align the gathered edge of the white fabric right sides together with one of the 20″ sides of the striped fabric. Sew, then press the seam to one side.

4. Fold the bag in half lengthwise, matching the seam. Sew, then press the seam to one side.

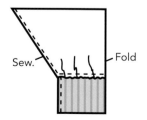

Sew side seam.

5. Align the bottom edges of the bag. Sew.

6. Spread open the bottom seam, and align it with the side seam. Measure 2″ in from the corner point, and sew across the base. Backstitch at the starting and stopping points. Repeat for the other side, aligning the bottom seam with the middle of the side.

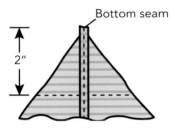

Bottom seam

2″

Sew across base.

7. Fold and press a double 1″ hem along the top (white) edge of the bag.

8. Topstitch the hem in place, leaving a 1″ opening in the middle of 1 side. Backstitch at the starting and stopping points.

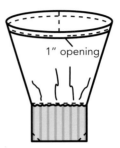

1″ opening

Topstitch hem.

9. Turn the bag right-side out.

10. Thread the ribbon through the hem at the top of the bag. Sew a large button to each end of the ribbon to keep the ends from getting lost inside the hem when the bag is open.

11. Sew decorative buttons to the white icing. Use white thread to attach the buttons so that the thread does not show through from the back of the fabric to the front.

tip: The tote bag can be stuffed with polyester fiberfill and used as a bed pillow.

Robo-Cupcake and Friends

MADE BY: Casey Dukes
FINISHED SIZE: approximately 5½″ × 6½″, including head and limbs

Ingredients

Polka dot fabric: 2 squares 3″ × 3″

Solid fabric: 2 pieces 4″ × 3″

fast2fuse Double-Sided Fusible Stiff Interfacing (heavyweight): 1 piece 3″ × 3″ and 1 piece 4″ × 3″

Fantastiques *by Trice Boerens* (available at craft stores or at www.ctpub.com) or other source of arms, legs, and heads

Embroidery floss

Fabric glue

Instructions

1. Trace the cupcake bottom pattern (page 115) on 1 piece of polka dot fabric. Trace the cupcake top pattern (page 115) on 1 piece of solid fabric. **Lightly** mark the dashed line with a pencil.

2. On the cupcake top, hand stitch a running stitch along the dashed line with 2 or 3 strands of embroidery floss to cover the pencil line.

3. With a hot iron, adhere the polka dot fabric to both sides of the 3″ × 3″ piece of fast2fuse. Adhere the solid fabric to the 4″ × 3″ piece of fast2fuse. Use a nonstick cloth to protect the ironing board.

4. Trim along the marked pattern lines.

5. Using fabric glue, adhere the top and bottom pieces of the cupcake so that the top overlaps the bottom by ½″ or so. Then adhere the head and limbs to the finished cupcake.

Cutie Cupcake Ponytail Holder

MADE BY: Kerry Graham
FINISHED SIZE: approximately 2″ × 1¾″

Ingredients

Wool roving

Felting needle

Stretchy hair band

Plastic soda or water bottle cap

White acrylic paint

Pearl lustre paint

Sparkle glaze

Mod Podge

Gloss varnish

Craft glue

Craft knife

Sequins, beads, buttons

Instructions

1. Roll a good handful of wool roving into a loose ball. Needle felt the ball until it is firm.

2. Embellish with sequins, beads, and buttons. Use a needle and thread to go from the bottom of the roving through to the top. Make sure that any loose threads will be hidden when pushed into the bottle cap.

3. Cut a hole ¼″ × ⅛″ into the center of the bottle cap. It should be just large enough to push the hair band through so that it fits snugly inside.

4. Paint the bottle cap white. Let it dry. Repeat. This will take a couple of coats if the bottle cap has printed text on it. Cover with Mod Podge to seal the paint. When dry, paint with pearl lustre. When dry, paint with sparkle glaze. Once you have a nice look for your cupcake holder, paint with gloss varnish for a protective finish. Allow it to dry.

5. Squeeze the hair band into the hole in the bottle cap.

6. Place a lot of glue inside the bottle cap—use enough to cover the hair band so that it does not come out and to cover the inside so that the cupcake top can be glued in.

7. Firmly press the embellished cupcake top into the bottle cap. Allow the glue to dry completely before using.

Cupcake **Magic Wands**

MADE BY: Jane Dávila
FINISHED SIZE: 4˝ × 11½˝

Ingredients

For each cupcake wand, you'll need the following:

Scraps of 3 different solid or solid-like cotton fabrics

Backing fabric: 4¹/2˝ × 7˝

fast2fuse Double-Sided Fusible Stiff Interfacing (heavyweight): 4½˝ × 7˝

³/16˝ dowel: 9˝ long

Acrylic paint: your choice of 2 colors

Paintbrush

Fabric glue

Pencil

½˝-wide masking tape

Instructions

1. Trace the pattern on page 118, and use it to cut out 1 cupcake bottom, 1 cupcake top, and 1 cherry from fast2fuse.

2. Iron the selected fabric to one side of each of the fast2fuse pieces. Use a nonstick cloth to protect the ironing board. Cut them out, using the fast2fuse as a guide.

3. Sew around the perimeter of the cherry, the cupcake top piece, and the cupcake base.

4. Draw the pleat lines on the cupcake bottom very lightly with a pencil.

5. Sew the pleat lines on the cupcake bottom.

6. Iron the backing fabric to the back of each of your cupcake pieces. Trim the backing fabric, using the fast2fuse as a guide.

7. Use fabric glue to attach the cupcake pieces together, overlapping the pieces slightly. Set aside to dry.

8. Paint the dowel with your first color, and allow paint to dry.

9. Wrap ½"-wide masking tape around the dowel about every ½" to form stripes. Paint the open stripes with the other color paint. Allow paint to dry, and remove the tape.

10. Place the completed cupcake facedown on the table. Glue the dowel in place with the fabric glue.

 tip: For good adhesion, place a weight on top of the dowel while the glue dries.

 tip: Add trailing ribbons to use the cupcake wands as magic wands, or use as part of a table setting, place setting, or bouquet.

Ode to **Cupcakes Shrine**

MADE BY: Jane Dávila
FINISHED SIZE: 11¼″ × 7¼″

Ingredients

Backing fabric: ¼ yard

Background fabric: ¼ yard

Assorted fabric: scraps for cupcake, letters, and word backgrounds

fast2fuse Double-Sided Stiff Interfacing (heavyweight): 12″ × 8″

Paper-backed fusible web, 17″ wide: ¼ yard

¾-high alphabet stamps

Fabric ink stamp pad

Glass beads in assorted colors

Beading thread and beading needle

Silver glitter finish

Metallic paint

Paintbrush

Legal size plain white paper

Instructions

1. From plain paper, cut a rectangle 2½″ × 5¼″. Fold it in half widthwise, and trace the curve pattern (page 116). Cut out the shape.

2. Draw lines on a 7¼″ × 11¼″ sheet of paper as shown. Use the curve pattern from Step 1 to draw the curve.

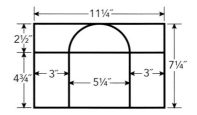

Create pattern.

3. Cut out the shrine pattern, trace it onto the fast2fuse, and cut out the fast2fuse.

4. Iron the background fabric to the cut-out fast2fuse shrine. Use a nonstick cloth to protect the ironing board. Trim away the excess, using the fast2fuse as a guide.

5. Draw lines from the curved section down to the bottom, forming 2 side and 1 center panel.

6. Sew along drawn lines between center and side panels and just to either side of each drawn line, for a total of 3 rows of stitching at each line.

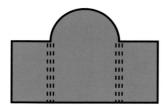

Sew panel divider lines.

7. Draw 1 rectangle 3½″ × 4½″ and 2 rectangles 1½″ × 3″ on fusible web. Also trace each cupcake part and the letters Y-U-M on the fusible web. (*Note: Patterns are on pages 116–117. Letters are reversed for appliqué.*) Cut out each fusible web shape with a wide margin, being careful not to cut directly on the lines.

8. Iron the cut-out fusible web pieces onto the back of each chosen fabric. Cut out each piece directly on the line, and peel off the paper backing.

9. Using alphabet stamps and fabric stamp pad, stamp the word SWEET onto a 1½″ × 3″ background rectangle and TASTY onto the other.

10. Using the photo (page 18) for placement, iron the pieces in place on the fast2fuse shrine.

11. Topstitch around the 3 rectangles.

12. Stitch twice around each letter of YUM.

13. Stitch twice around each cupcake part and on the pleat lines on the cupcake base.

14. Iron the backing fabric to the back of the shrine. Cut away the excess fabric.

15. Topstitch around the perimeter of the shrine.

16. Sew beads on the 2 side panels with beading thread and a beading needle. Keep beads at least ¼″ away from the outside edges and the drawn lines.

17. Use a small paintbrush and metallic paint to coat the outside edges of the shrine to finish raw edges and to add a touch of color and sheen.

18. Use a small paintbrush to add a small amount of silver glitter finish to the cupcake frosting.

19. After all of the paint is dry, fold in the side panels slightly along the stitched lines to allow the shrine to stand unsupported.

Sweet Strawberry **Cupcake Purses**

MADE BY: Zinnia Heinzmann
FINISHED SIZES: 9″ × 10″ (purse), 5″ × 5½″ (mini purse)

Ingredients

Strawberry pink cotton fabric: 1 fat quarter

Chocolate brown cotton fabric: 1 fat quarter

White cotton flannel: 1 fat quarter (used instead of batting)

Decorative ribbon: 1″ wide for purse, 1 yard; ½″ wide for mini purse, ¼ yard

Assorted buttons and/or beads

Light pink embroidery floss

Golden-brown thread or floss for hand stitching

Chalk pencil

¼″-diameter sew-on snaps (optional): 3

Instructions

Note: Seam allowances are ¼″.

1. Enlarge the patterns as directed (page 121); cut the strawberry pink fabric into 2 frosting shapes and 2 whole cupcake shapes.

2. Cut the chocolate brown fabric into 2 cupcake bottom shapes, using the pattern, and 1 rectangle 4⅝″ × 23″ (for the purse) or 3¼″ × 15½″ (for the mini purse).

3. Cut the white flannel into 2 whole cupcake shapes.

4. To assemble the cupcake front, sew a frosting shape to a cupcake bottom shape, right sides together. Press the seam allowance toward the cupcake bottom. Repeat for the cupcake back.

5. To make the front pocket piece, turn under and press a ¼″ double hem along the top long edge of the chocolate brown rectangle from Step 2. Press ½″ pleats across the rectangle. Using the golden-brown thread, hand or machine stitch vertically along each pleat, anchoring it in place. Your finished pocket piece should measure at least 4⅛" × 7¼" (purse) or 2¾" × 4⅝" (mini purse).

Pleat and stitch pocket fabric.

6. Pin the pocket to the cupcake front, both with right sides up, matching the hemmed pocket top to the center cupcake seam on the cupcake front. Trim the excess pocket fabric to the edge of the cupcake front.

7. Layer a flannel whole cupcake piece, the cupcake front (right-side up with pocket pinned in place), the cupcake back (right-side down) and the last flannel whole cupcake piece on top. Pin or baste. Sew together the layers, leaving the top of the cupcake open. Trim the excess seam allowance at the bottom cupcake corners.

8. Fold and press the front and back frosting top seam allowance out toward the white flannel, clipping into the seam allowance as needed for smooth curves.

9. To attach the strap, whipstitch each end of the ribbon to the flannel on the cupcake back at each end of the cupcake opening. (For the mini purse, stitch the 2 ends of the ribbon together at the same side of the opening.)

Folded seam
allowance

Flannel

Stitch ribbon to flannel on cupcake back.

10. Turn the cupcake right-side out. Use a chalk pencil to draw the frosting swirls on the cupcake front as in the photo (page 26). Hand quilt, using the light pink embroidery floss.

11. Embellish the front cupcake frosting with buttons and/or beads.

12. To make the lining, pin and sew the 2 strawberry pink whole cupcake shapes together. Trim the excess seam allowance at the bottom cupcake corners. Fold and press the frosting top seam allowance outward, clipping into the seam allowance as needed for smooth curves.

13. Insert the lining into the cupcake. Pin, and blindstitch the lining along the cupcake opening to secure it in place.

14. For added stability, backstitch each edge of the ribbon strap along the cupcake opening, using the light pink embroidery floss.

15. To add snaps, mark a dot for each snap on the lining front and back along the cupcake opening. Hand stitch each snap in place.

tip: For a delectable evening purse, use silks, taffeta, or other dressy fabrics for the cupcake frosting and bottom pieces instead of the cotton. Sew crystals or semiprecious stone beads to the frosting. Add satin ribbons or other fancy embellishments as you wish. For the perfect wristlet, measure the ribbon strap so that it fits nicely around your wrist, and attach as instructed.

Tiny Treasure **Cupcake Pins**

MADE BY: Mary Link
FINISHED SIZE: about 1" × 1"

Ingredients

Fabric: scraps

fast2fuse Double-Sided Fusible Stiff Interfacing (regular or heavyweight): scraps

Embellishments of choice, such as glitter or pompoms

Pin back

Glue

Water-based gloss varnish

Instructions

1. Use the pattern of your choice from pages 122–124, and reduce it to about 1" × 1".

2. Cut out the fast2fuse, using the reduced pattern.

3. Iron fabric to both sides of the fast2fuse. Use a non-stick cloth to protect the ironing board. Trim, using the fast2fuse as a guide.

4. Embellish and coat with several layers of gloss varnish.

5. Glue a pin back to the back of the cupcake.

 tip: These tiny treasures make great magnets, too. Just glue a magnet to the back instead of a pin back.

Charming Cupcake **Bracelet**

MADE BY: Jane Dávila
FINISHED SIZE: 3" diameter

Ingredients

Grafix Shrink Film, either white or inkjet printable (available from www.countryquilter.com)

Felted wool beads

Assorted beads: glass, wood, and plastic in various sizes and colors

Elastic bead cord

Scissors for cutting shrink film

1/4" hole punch

Superglue or clear nail polish

Small jump rings

Jewelry pliers

Markers and fine-grit sandpaper (if using white shrink film)

Scanner and inkjet printer (if using inkjet printable shrink film)

Instructions

CUPCAKE CHARMS

1. Prepare the shrink film as follows:

If you are using inkjet printable shrink film, scan the 4 cupcakes (page 119) into your computer, and print them onto the shrink film. Allow the film to dry.

If you are using white shrink film, trace the cupcake shape (page 119) onto shrink film 4 times with black marker. Color in each section of cupcake with colored markers, following drawings for color suggestions. Allow the film to dry.

2. Cut out each cupcake approximately 1/16" away from the outside edge. Punch a 1/4" hole about 1/4" from the top edge. Follow the manufacturer's instructions to shrink the film.

BRACELET

1. Use jewelry pliers to attach a jump ring through the hole at the top of each cupcake.

2. Cut a length of elastic bead cord about 10″ long.

3. Lay out the beads in a circle in a pleasing pattern, evenly spacing the cupcakes around the circle.

4. Thread the elastic beading cord through the beads, one at a time. Make sure that all the cupcakes are facing the same direction.

5. Pull both ends of the elastic beading cord until the first bead and the last bead meet. Tie the 2 ends in a square knot. Use superglue or clear nail polish to seal the knot. Trim the excess cord.

More Than Just a **Cupcake Book**

MADE BY: Sue Astroth
FINISHED SIZE: 7½" × 10"

Ingredients

2 coordinating fabrics: 16" × 11" each
(1 fat quarter each)

Paper-backed fusible web, 17" wide: 1 yard

*Plain paper, 1 piece 11" × 16" and 1 piece
4" × 4"* for lining

Pink fabric: 2 scraps 4" × 4"

White Fun Flock (from Stampendous)

Paper adhesive

Fabric adhesive such as Fabri-Tac

Flower (from Queen and Company)

Brad (from Limited Edition)

Ribbon, ½" wide: 1 yard

Tapestry needle, size 24

Bone folder

Waxed linen thread: ½ yard in 1 or 2 colors

Cardstock: 6" × 6" pieces in colors to
match fabric

Textured white paper: 2 or 3 sheets, 19" × 25"
for book pages

Craft knife such as X-ACTO

2¾" Circle #3 die cut (from Sizzix; optional)

3¾" Scallop square die cut (from Quickutz;
optional)

Cupcake die cut (from Quickutz; optional)

Screw punch (optional)

Instructions

1. Iron fusible web to the wrong side of the
16" × 11" coordinating fabrics. When cool,
remove the paper backing, and fuse the fabric
to both sides of the 16" × 11" lining paper.

2. When cool, cut the prepared fabric/paper
to 15" × 10". This is the book cover. Use a bone
folder to fold the book cover in half so that it
measures 7½" × 10". Unfold.

3. Finish the edges of the cover using a decorative stitch. Start and end the stitching at the fold.

4. Iron fusible web to the wrong side of the pink scraps. Remove the paper backing, and fuse the pink fabric scraps to both sides of the 4″ × 4″ lining paper. Cut out a 2¾″ circle. Finish around the edge of the circle using a decorative stitch.

 tip: A die cutter makes quick work of cutting shapes like the circle, scallop, and cupcake shape. If you don't have a die cutter, just cut the shapes with a scissors or craft knife.

5. Cut out a cupcake (use a die cut, a pattern from pages 122–124, or design your own), a 3½″ scallop square, and a 3″ × 3″ square from cardstock.

6. Center the straight-edged square on the scallop square. On the sewing machine, sew them together using a slightly meandering stitch. Use the photo as your guide.

7. Cover the frosting part of the cupcake completely with a light coating of adhesive, and then apply flocking. Let dry. Add flower and brad.

8. Assemble and layer the cupcake on the finished pink circle, and glue in place.

9. Using the photo as your guide, glue the pink circle to the layered squares, and then glue the complete embellishment to the book cover. Let it dry.

10. Cut textured white paper into 4–6 sheets, each 14″ × 9½″. Fold the sheets in half with a bone folder so that they measure 7″ × 9½″. Stack them together, fold, and trim if necessary.

11. Stack the cover and pages.

12. Make 4 holes along the fold at the following increments: 1½″ and 4″ from both the top and bottom edges.

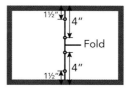

Make holes along fold.

13. Using 2 strands of the waxed linen thread and a tapestry needle, start from inside the book and take the needle through the top hole. Bring the needle in through the second hole. Tie off. Repeat for the bottom 2 holes.

14. Wrap the brown ribbon around the front cover, and tie into a bow.

Delightful Cupcake **Book Cover**

MADE BY: Jake Finch
FINISHED SIZE: 10″ × 10″ closed; 10″ × 22″ open

Ingredients

8″ × 8″ post bound scrapbook

fast2fuse Double-Sided Fusible Stiff Interfacing (regular weight): 1 piece 10″ × 22″ (1 fat quarter)

Brown fabric: 1 piece 12″× 24″ for inside cover; 2 pieces 17″ × 10″ for sleeves; 1 piece 12″ × 17″ and 1 piece 12″ × 4″ for the outside cover (³/4 yard)

Pink fabric: 5″ × 5″ scrap for cover

Tan fabric: 6″ × 6″ scrap for cover

Brown, white, and tan fabrics: 2″ × 3¹/2″ scrap of each for cupcake

White fabric: 1 piece 12″ by 3¹/2″ for cover

Cotton batting: 12″ × 24″

Buttons and beads for embellishment

¹/2–1 yard ribbon for closure

10″ ribbon for embellishment

Lightweight fusible inter-facing (22″ wide): ⁵/8 yard (the kind used in garment construction)

Paper-backed fusible web (17″ wide): ¹/3 yard

505 Spray and Fix temporary fabric adhesive (optional)

Fabric glue (optional)

Instructions

1. Fuse the 12″ × 24″ brown fabric to 1 side of the fast2fuse, following the manufacturer's directions. Trim the fabric to the edge of the fast2fuse. This is the inside of the cover.

2. Fold the fast2fuse in half, and mark the center. Draw a line from the top to the bottom through the center mark. Draw 4 lines, spaced ¼″ apart, on both sides of the center line.

3. Stitch along each drawn line. Make sure your bobbin thread matches the fabric.

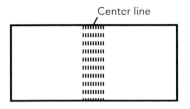

Stitch center lines.

4. Fuse the lightweight interfacing to the wrong sides of each 17″ × 10″ brown fabric sleeve piece. Fold the sleeves wrong sides together in half so that each measures 8½″ × 10″. Press well.

5. Position a sleeve on the fabric side of the fast2fuse cover, aligning the raw edges of the sleeve with the edges at one end of the cover. The sleeve fold will be 8½″ toward the center of the cover. Pin in place, and then baste with a ⅛″ seam allowance along the 3 edges of the

cover. Repeat for the second sleeve at the other end of the cover.

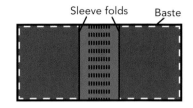

Baste sleeves to fabric side of fast2fuse cover.

6. To make the quilted outside of the cover, align the 12″ sides of the 12″ × 17″ piece of brown fabric and the 12″ × 3½″ piece of white fabric. Sew together with a ¼″ seam allowance. Press the seam toward the brown fabric. Then sew the 12″ × 4″ piece of brown fabric to the other 12″ side of the white fabric. Press the seam toward the brown fabric.

7. Place the embellishment ribbon down the center of the white fabric. Pin in place, and stitch down with matching thread.

8. Iron the fusible web to the back of the 6″ × 6″ tan and 5″ × 5″ pink scraps. Remove the backing paper, and layer the tan and then the pink onto the center of the white section of the front cover, as shown in the photo (page 26). Fuse into place.

9. Use the patterns on page 120 to trace the cupcake pieces onto the paper side of the fusible web. Roughly cut out the patterns, and fuse them to the wrong side of the selected fabric scraps. Trim the shapes along the traced lines, layer, and fuse on the center of the pink square.

10. Satin stitch around the edge of the tan square, and use a decorative stitch around the edge of the pink square. Stitch fold lines onto the cupcake wrapper, and outline the cake and frosting.

11. Use 505 Spray and Fix temporary fabric adhesive, hand basting stitches, or basting pins to baste the batting to the wrong side of the outside cover. Quilt as desired. Remove basting as necessary.

12. Trim the outside cover to 10″ × 22″, and embellish.

13. To join the outside cover to the inside cover, heavily spray-baste or glue the batting side of the outside cover to the fast2fuse side of the inside. Carefully center the outside on the inside, making sure everything is lined up, and smooth in place. Cut 2 lengths of ribbon for the closure, and slip each end about 4″ between the cover's front and back at the center of each 10″ side.

14. Round the corners of the cover, using a spool as a cutting guide. Satin stitch around the outside edges to finish.

tip: Plan to satin stitch around the cover twice to get smooth, complete stitching coverage.

Cupcake **Lacing Toy**

MADE BY: Mary Link
FINISHED SIZES: approximately 6″ × 6″ to 8″ × 8″

Ingredients

note: Adjust amounts as needed if you enlarge the pattern past 8″ × 8″. For each toy, you'll need the following:

Fabric: scraps for cupcake bottom, top, and backing

fast2fuse Double-Sided Fusible Stiff Interfacing (heavyweight): 8″ × 8″

Cording: 24″

Embellishments of choice (glitter, rickrack, chenille strips, or pompoms)

Glue

Water-based gloss varnish for a durable finish (optional)

Hole punch for paper

Tape

Instructions

1. Use the pattern on page 125, and enlarge as desired.

2. For each toy, cut 1 whole cupcake shape from fast2fuse.

3. Iron fabric to the back of the fast2fuse. Trim, using the fast2fuse as a guide. Cut out fabric for the cupcake top and bottom, and fuse to the other side of the fast2fuse.

4. Coat with a layer of varnish (optional).

5. Punch holes approximately 1″ apart around the cupcake.

6. Embellish as desired.

7. Tie a knot at an end of the cording, and wrap the other end with tape to make a "needle." Lace through the first hole of the cupcake.

My Little **Cupcake Card**

MADE BY: Sue Astroth
FINISHED SIZE: 5″ × 7″

Ingredients

Polka dot fabric: 2 pieces 11″ × 8″
(1 fat quarter)

Plain paper for lining: 1 piece 11″ × 8″
and 1 piece 4″ × 4″

Paper-backed fusible web 17″ wide:
³/₄ yard

Pink fabric: 2 scraps, 4″ × 4″ each

*Scraps from cupcake fabric (you could
also use stickers or die cuts)*

Fabric adhesive such as Fabri-Tac

Pink ribbon: 10″–12″ scrap

Cardstock: 5″ × 7″ pieces of turquoise
and white

Text cardstock: 8¹/₂″ × 11″ piece

Craft knife such as X-ACTO

Bone folder

2³/₄″ Circle #3 die cut (from Sizzix;
optional)

3¹/₂″ Scallop frame die cut (from
Quickutz; optional)

Instructions

1. Iron fusible web to the wrong side of the fabric.

2. When cool, remove the paper backing, and fuse the fabric to both sides of the 11″ × 8″ lining paper.

3. When cool, cut the prepared fabric/paper to 10″ × 7″. This is the card cover.

4. Use a bone folder to fold the card cover in half so it measures 5″ × 7″. Unfold.

5. Finish the edges of the card with a decorative stitch. Start and end the stitching at the fold.

6. Iron the fusible web to the wrong side of the pink fabric scraps.

7. When cool, remove the paper backing, and fuse the fabric scraps to the 4″ × 4″ lining paper.

8. Cut out a 2¾″ circle from the pink fabric/paper.

9. Finish around the edge of the circle with a decorative stitch.

10. Iron fusible web to the wrong side of the cupcake fabric scraps. Cut out 2 cupcakes.

11. Fuse 1 cupcake cutout to the pink circle.

 tip: Make text cardstock using a computer and word processing software. Create a document in your favorite font, repeating the phrase "my little cupcake" (you could also use a name, favorite saying, "celebrate"... you get the idea). Print the text on 8½ × 11-inch lightweight cardstock.

12. Cut out a scallop frame. Cut a piece of the text cardstock to fit behind the opening of the frame.

13. Glue the text cardstock, frame, and circle to the front of the card.

14. Make a small bow, and glue it in place.

15. For the inside of the card, cut white cardstock to 4" × 6". Iron on the second fabric cupcake in lower right corner. Layer and glue white cardstock onto turquoise cardstock, trim to fit in the card, and glue it in place.

 tip: A die cutter makes quick work of cutting shapes like the circle, scallop, and cupcake shape. If you don't have a die cutter, just cut the shapes with a scissors or craft knife.

Use-for-Anything
Cupcake **Embellishments**

MADE BY: Kerry Graham
FINISHED SIZE: approximately 2¼″ × 2″

Ingredients

Various colors of felt

Beads, sequins, and other embellishments

Fabric glue

Instructions

 tip: Before you start cutting, make a few copies of the cupcake illustrations you want to use, and color them in to get an idea of how your cupcake will look.

1. Use any of the cupcake patterns on pages 122–124. Reduce or enlarge them to meet your needs.

2. Make templates of the cupcakes you want to use, and trace them onto felt.

3. Cut out the felt pieces. *Note: Be sure to cut the cupcake bottom about ¼″ higher at the top to allow the cupcake top to overlap when gluing.*

4. Cut a felt backing piece that is about ¼″ to ½″ larger than the template all around. Once your cupcake front is finished, you will glue it to the backing, and then trim the backing to be about ⅛″ larger than the front, providing an outline.

5. Glue the cupcake pieces together.

6. Glue on the backing. When the glue is dry, trim the backing.

7. Embellish as desired.

 tip: Use for hair barrettes, headbands, embellishments for clothes, or anything that needs a little sweetening up.

 tip: When using these cupcakes as clothing embellishments, sew a snap to the clothing and to the cupcakes so you have detachable and interchangeable embellishments. Remove the embellishments before washing.

recipes and decorating ideas

surprise cupcakes

Liz Aneloski

The surprise is a yummy center of cream cheese and chocolate chips. These are so good that they don't even need frosting; but just in case you want to frost them, there's a scrumptious (and easy) chocolate frosting recipe that follows.

Ingredients

Makes 2 dozen cupcakes.

CUPCAKES

1 package of chocolate cake mix (*Note: Do not use a cake mix with pudding in the mix because the filling will not sink into the cupcake.*)

FILLING

8 ounces cream cheese

⅓ cup sugar

1 egg

6 ounces chocolate chips

Directions

1. Mix the cake mix according to the package instructions.

2. Line muffin pans with paper baking cups, and fill ⅔ full.

3. Mix the cream cheese and sugar. Beat in the egg, and stir in the chocolate chips.

4. Drop 1 rounded teaspoon of filling into each cupcake.

5. Bake as directed on the cake mix package for cupcakes.

chocolate frosting

Lynn Koolish

Dark and rich, this frosting is as delicious as it is easy to make.
You probably have everything you need in the pantry.

Ingredients

- 1 stick (8 tablespoons) melted butter
- ¾ cup unsweetened cocoa powder
- 3 cups powdered sugar
- ¼ cup milk
- 1 teaspoon vanilla

Directions

1. Sift the cocoa powder and powdered sugar together.

2. Combine all the ingredients and beat until smooth. If frosting is too thick,
add a bit more milk. If frosting is too thin, add a bit more powdered sugar.

classic white cupcakes

Sandy Bonsib

The name says it all—these cupcakes are a classic.
Match them with any frosting for a real treat.

Ingredients

Makes 1½ dozen cupcakes.

2 cups white flour

1½ cups sugar

1 tablespoon baking powder

1 teaspoon salt

1 cup milk

½ cup shortening

2 teaspoons vanilla extract

4 egg whites

Directions

Preheat oven to 350°.

1. In a mixing bowl, stir together the flour, sugar, baking powder, and salt.
Add the milk, shortening, and vanilla. Beat with an electric mixer on low speed
until combined. Then beat on medium speed for 2 minutes.

2. Add unbeaten egg whites. Beat on medium speed for 2 minutes, scraping the
sides of the bowl frequently.

3. Line muffin pans with paper baking cups, and fill ½ full.

4. Bake at 350° for 20 minutes or until done.

creamy frosting

Sandy Bonsib

This is the perfect frosting for decorating because you can make it any color you like. Try using gel food coloring—you can make colors ranging from pale pastel to dark and bright.

Ingredients

1½ cups shortening (use Crisco if you want to keep the frosting white)

1 teaspoon almond extract

5½–6 cups powdered sugar

¼–⅓ cup milk

Directions

1. In a mixing bowl, beat the shortening and almond extract with an electric mixer on medium speed for about 30 seconds.

2. Gradually add about half of the powdered sugar, beating well.

3. Add ¼ cup of milk.

4. Gradually beat in the remaining powdered sugar and enough of the remaining milk to make the frosting a spreading consistency.

5. Add food coloring if you like.

chocolate decadence cupcakes

Sandy Bonsib

These are the best—dark, rich, and dense. Truly decadent.

Ingredients

Makes 2½ dozen cupcakes.

2 cups semisweet chocolate chips

6 ounces unsweetened chocolate

¾ cup butter

⅔ cup flour

½ teaspoon baking powder

½ teaspoon salt

6 eggs

2 cups sugar

4 teaspoons vanilla extract

Directions

Preheat oven to 350°.

1. Melt the semisweet chocolate chips, unsweetened chocolate, and butter in the microwave or in a saucepan over low heat. Stir until smooth.

2. In a mixing bowl, combine the flour, baking powder, and salt.

3. In a large mixing bowl, beat the eggs, sugar, and vanilla until fluffy. Beat in the cooled chocolate mixture. Add the flour mixture, and mix until combined. Chill until the batter mounds with a spoon.

4. Line muffin pans with paper baking cups, and fill ½ full.

5. Bake at 350° for 22 minutes. Test with a toothpick for doneness; do not overbake.

decadent topping

Sandy Bonsib

This foamy whipped cream is the perfect counterpoint to the rich, dark chocolate of the Chocolate Decadence Cupcakes.

Ingredients

1 cup heavy whipping cream

1 tablespoon sugar

1 teaspoon vanilla

Directions

1. Whip the heavy whipping cream until it mounds slightly.

2. Add the sugar and vanilla, and whip until peaks hold their shape.

ice-cream cone cupcakes

Mary Stori

Kids can't believe these cupcakes are actually baked in ice-cream cones—have the kids help you in the kitchen to bake them. Then they can have a blast decorating them.

Ingredients

Makes 1 dozen cupcakes.

1¼ cups flour

1 cup sugar

1½ teaspoons baking powder

½ teaspoon salt

¾ cup milk

⅓ cup shortening

1 egg

1 teaspoon vanilla

12 large, flat-bottom ice-cream cones

Directions

Preheat oven to 375°.

1. Measure all the ingredients (except the cones) into a large bowl.

2. Beat together, using an electric mixer. Start on low speed for 30 seconds, scrape the bowl, and beat for 3 minutes on high.

3. Place the ice-cream cones on a baking sheet. Spoon the batter into the cones, filling them only ½ full. *Note: Do not fill cones more than ½ full.*

4. Bake at 375° for 15–20 minutes or until done.

peppermint frosting

Mary Stori

Crushed peppermint candy gives this frosting a sweet crunch.
Tint the frosting pink to complete the look.

Ingredients

⅓ cup softened butter

3 tablespoons milk

3 cups sifted powdered sugar

¼–½ teaspoon peppermint extract

¼ teaspoon vanilla extract

Crushed, hard peppermint candy

Food coloring (optional)

Directions

1. In a mixing bowl, combine the butter, the milk, and 1 cup of the sugar.
Beat until well mixed.

2. Beat in the remaining 2 cups of sugar until the mixture is creamy and fluffy.

3. Add in the peppermint and vanilla extracts (and food coloring if desired). Mix well.

4. Spread on cooled cupcakes, and sprinkle with crushed peppermint candy.

martha washington cupcakes

Sandy Bonsib

Here's a different approach to cupcakes. These cupcakes are filled with dried fruits and nuts and flavored with nutmeg and mace—a great autumn treat.

Ingredients

Makes 2 dozen cupcakes.

1 cup butter

5 eggs, separated

2 cups total of dried fruit
(apples, pears, apricots, cherries, blueberries)

¼ cup chopped or sliced almonds

1 cup sugar

1¼ cups flour

1 teaspoon ground mace

1¼ teaspoons ground nutmeg

1 ounce (⅛ cup) orange juice

Directions

Preheat oven to 350°.

1. Allow eggs and butter to warm to room temperature.

2. Chop the fruits and nuts.

3. Separate the eggs, and set the yolks aside.

4. Beat the egg whites until soft peaks form.

5. Cream the butter. Slowly add the butter to the egg whites.

6. Slowly add the sugar to the egg white and butter mixture.

7. Add the egg yolks.

8. Slowly add the flour, then the mace, nutmeg, and orange juice.

9. By hand, stir in the fruit and nuts.

10. Line muffin pans with paper baking cups, and fill ½–⅔ full.

11. Bake at 350° for about 20 minutes or until done.

cream cheese frosting #1

Sandy Bonsib

Here's a classic approach to cream cheese frosting. Use for the Martha Washington Cupcakes on page 92 or the Carrot Cake Cupcakes on page 96.

Ingredients

6 ounces softened cream cheese

2 tablespoons milk

2 teaspoons vanilla
pinch of salt

4–5 cups powdered sugar

Directions

1. Blend the cream cheese, milk, vanilla, and salt.

2. Gradually add the sugar, beating until the frosting is smooth and of spreading consistency.

3. If necessary, stir in additional milk, 1 tablespoon at a time.

minnie's 5-flavor (pound cake) cupcakes

Demetrice Patterson

What happens when you take an old family recipe for pound cake and use it for cupcakes? You get a sophisticated dessert with a unique blend of flavors. It's definitely not your typical cupcake. Glaze with the 6-Flavor Glaze on page 95, or frost with one of the frosting recipes.

Ingredients

Makes 2–3 dozen cupcakes.

- 2 sticks softened butter
- ½ cup vegetable shortening
- 3 cups sugar
- 5 eggs, beaten (room temperature)
- 3 cups all-purpose flour
- ½ teaspoon baking powder
- 1 cup milk
- 1 teaspoon coconut flavor
- 1 teaspoon rum flavor
- 1 teaspoon butter flavor
- 1 teaspoon lemon extract
- 1 teaspoon vanilla extract

Directions

Preheat oven to 325°.

1. Cream the butter, shortening, and sugar until light and fluffy.

2. Beat the eggs until they are lemon colored. Add to the butter mixture.

3. Combine flour and baking powder, and add to the creamed mixture alternately with milk. Stir in flavorings. Beat on high speed 1 minute to add volume.

4. Line muffin pans with paper baking cups, and fill ½–⅔ full. Drop the pans a couple times to remove air bubbles.

5. Bake at 325° for 20 minutes or until done.

6-flavor glaze

Demetrice Patterson

Pair this sweet glaze with Minnie's 5-Flavor Cupcakes for a unique dessert. Not for the kids—this is a more adult take on cupcakes.

Ingredients

1 cup sugar

½ cup water

1 teaspoon each coconut, rum, butter, lemon, vanilla, and almond flavor extracts

Directions

1. Combine ingredients in heavy saucepan.

2. Bring to boil, stirring until sugar has melted.

3. Pour half of the glaze over the cupcakes while they are still in the pan and the other half after they are removed.

carrot cake cupcakes

Lynn Koolish

Carrots add color and moisture to these delectable cupcakes.

Ingredients

Makes 1 dozen cupcakes.

½ cup butter

½ cup brown sugar

½ cup white sugar

2 eggs

1 teaspoon vanilla

1½ cups grated carrots

1 cup flour

1 teaspoon baking powder

1 teaspoon baking soda

1 teaspoon nutmeg

1 teaspoon cinnamon

½ teaspoon salt

Directions

Preheat oven to 350°.

1. Cream together the butter and the sugars.

2. Add the eggs and vanilla.

3. Add the carrots and all the dry ingredients.

4. Line muffin pans with paper baking cups, and fill ½–⅔ full.

5. Bake at 350° for 20 minutes or until done.

cream cheese frosting #2

Mary Wruck

This is the easiest cream cheese frosting recipe you'll ever see. Honey adds a unique flavor to a classic frosting.

Ingredients

8 ounces softened cream cheese

¼ cup honey

Directions

Mix the honey into the cream cheese.

decorating ideas

When it comes to decorating cupcakes, there's no end to your options. With just a few decorating supplies, you can make them plain or fancy, silly or serious. Have a cupcake decorating party, and let everyone join in on the fun.

template
patterns

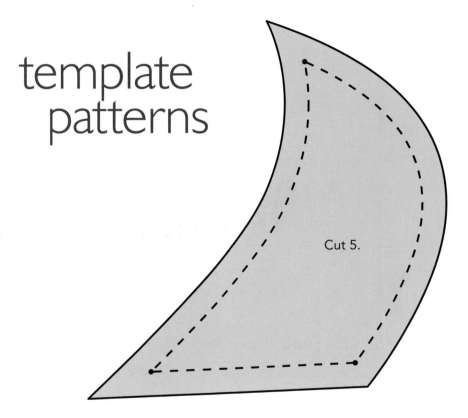

Cut 5.

ZERO-CALORIE FABRIC CUPCAKES

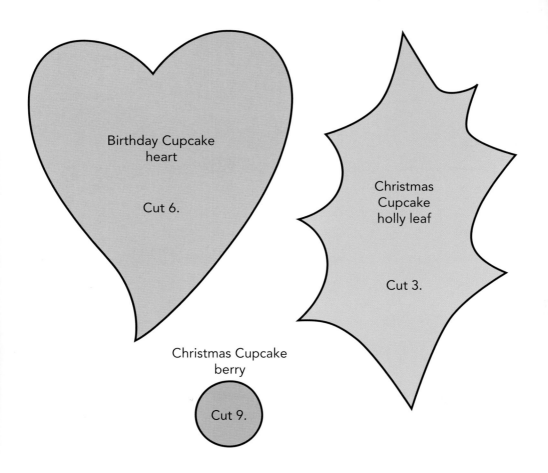

Birthday Cupcake
heart

Cut 6.

Christmas
Cupcake
holly leaf

Cut 3.

Christmas Cupcake
berry

Cut 9.

A TRIO OF FELTED CUPCAKES

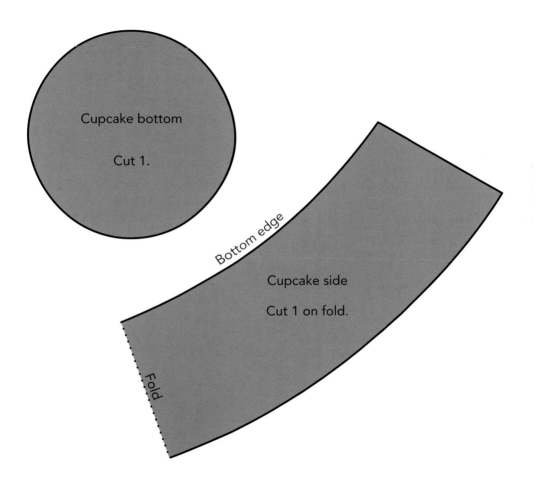

Cupcake bottom

Cut 1.

Bottom edge

Cupcake side

Cut 1 on fold.

Fold

CHOCOLATE CUPCAKE PINCUSHION

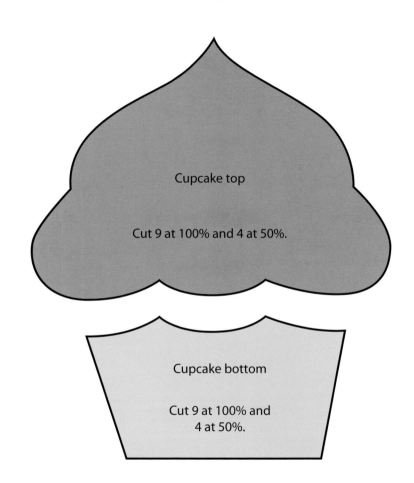

Cupcake top

Cut 9 at 100% and 4 at 50%.

Cupcake bottom

Cut 9 at 100% and
4 at 50%.

CUPCAKES! A MINI QUILT

THE DEFINITIVE HISTORY OF A CUPCAKE—PANEL 1

THE DEFINITIVE HISTORY OF A CUPCAKE—PANEL 2

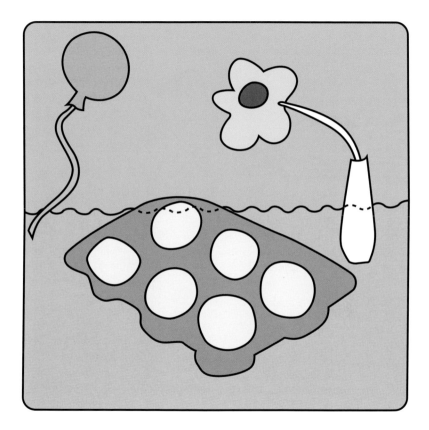

THE DEFINITIVE HISTORY OF A CUPCAKE—PANEL 3

THE DEFINITIVE HISTORY OF A CUPCAKE—PANEL 4

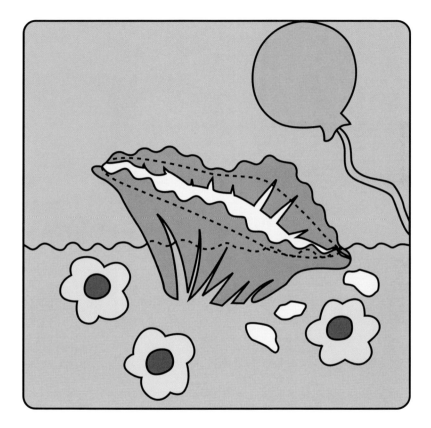

THE DEFINITIVE HISTORY OF A CUPCAKE—PANEL 5

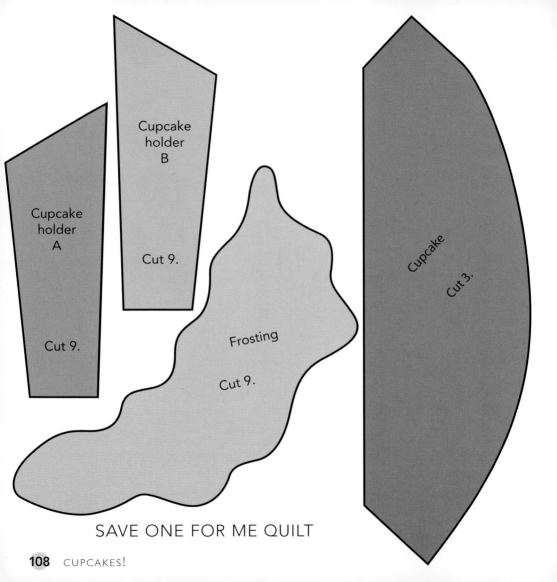

Cupcake holder A

Cut 9.

Cupcake holder B

Cut 9.

Frosting

Cut 9.

Cupcake

Cut 3.

SAVE ONE FOR ME QUILT

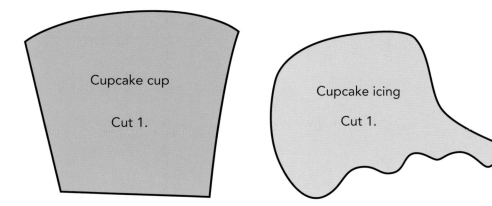

Cupcake cup

Cut 1.

Cupcake icing

Cut 1.

EAT DESSERT FIRST POSTCARD

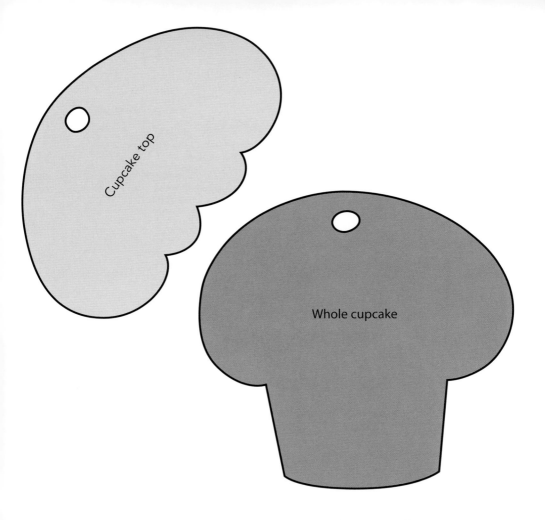

Cupcake top

Whole cupcake

IT'S A CUPCAKE PARTY INVITATION

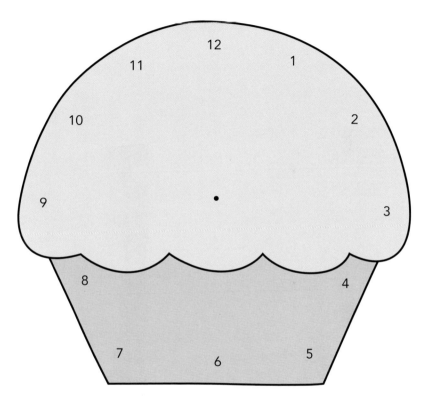

Enlarge 200%.

IT'S ALWAYS TIME FOR CUPCAKES CLOCK

Bead
placement

SWEET TREATS FRAMED CUPCAKE

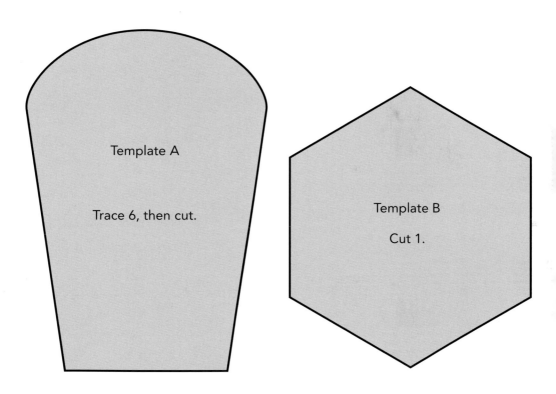

Template A

Trace 6, then cut.

Template B

Cut 1.

PETAL POT CUPCAKE CARRIER

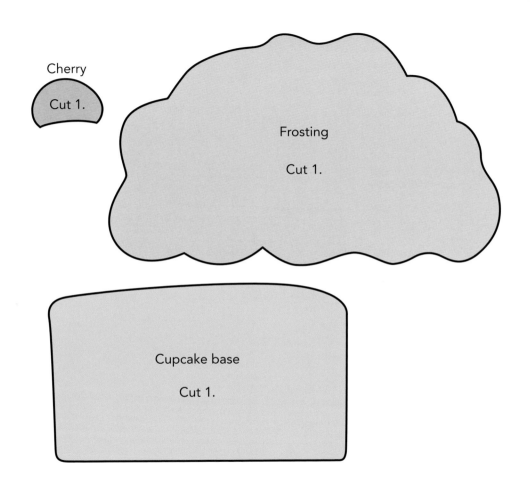

Cherry

Cut 1.

Frosting

Cut 1.

Cupcake base

Cut 1.

SARAH'S CUPPY CAKE PILLOW

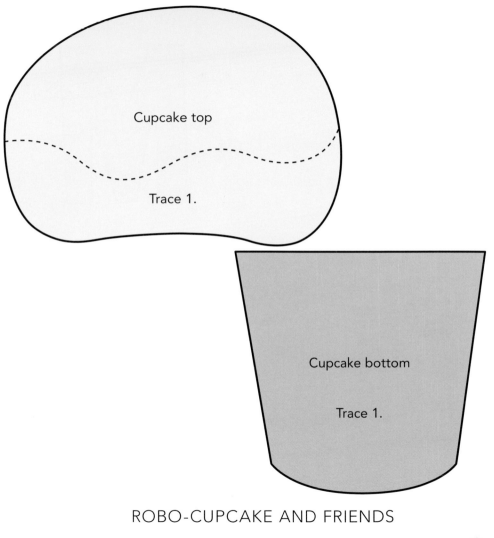

Cupcake top

Trace 1.

Cupcake bottom

Trace 1.

ROBO-CUPCAKE AND FRIENDS

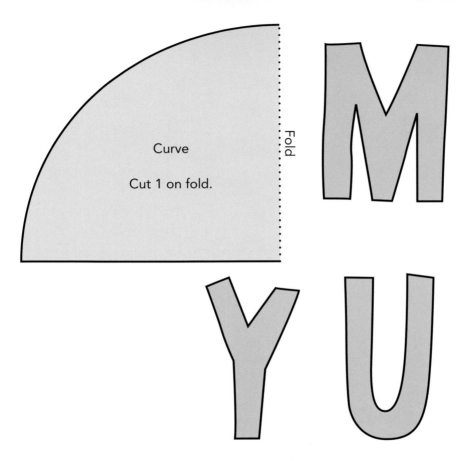

Curve

Cut 1 on fold.

Fold

Letters are reversed for appliqué. Cut 1 of each.

ODE TO CUPCAKES SHRINE

Pleat
lines

Cut 1 of each.

ODE TO CUPCAKES SHRINE

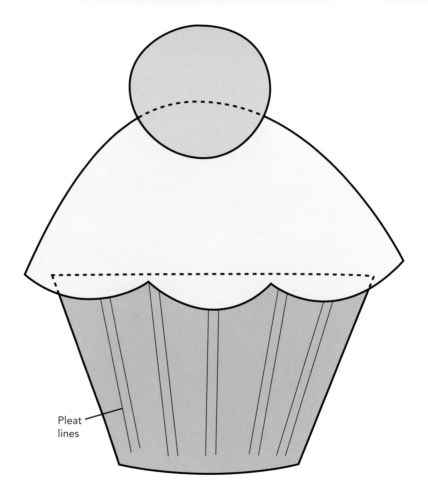

Pleat
lines

Cut 1 of each.

CUPCAKE MAGIC WANDS

CHARMING CUPCAKE BRACELET

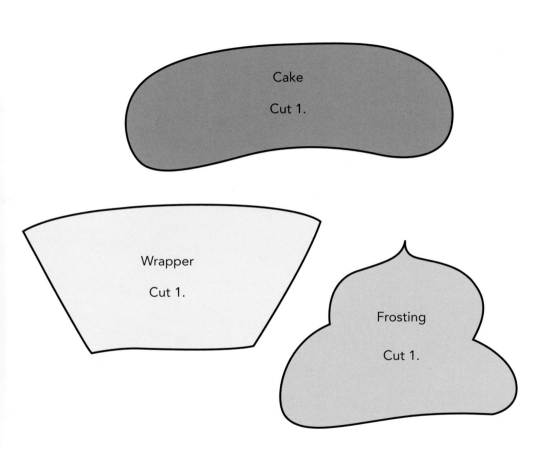

Cake

Cut 1.

Wrapper

Cut 1.

Frosting

Cut 1.

DELIGHTFUL CUPCAKE BOOK COVER

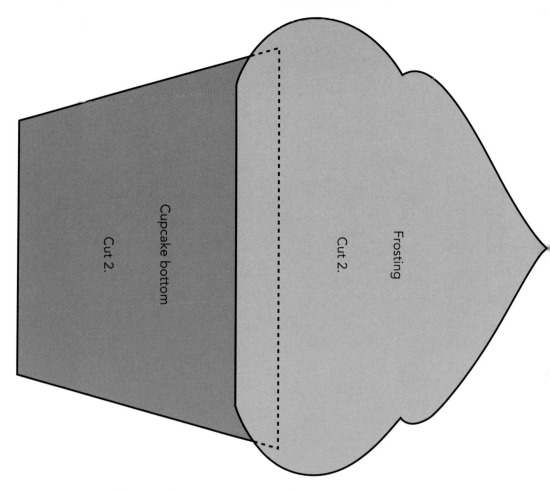

Cupcake bottom

Cut 2.

Frosting

Cut 2.

Enlarge 114% for the mini purse or 195% for the purse. Cut 4 of whole cupcake.

SWEET STRAWBERRY CUPCAKE PURSES

USE-FOR-ANYTHING CUPCAKE EMBELLISHMENTS

USE-FOR-ANYTHING CUPCAKE EMBELLISHMENTS

Backing

USE-FOR-ANYTHING CUPCAKE EMBELLISHMENTS

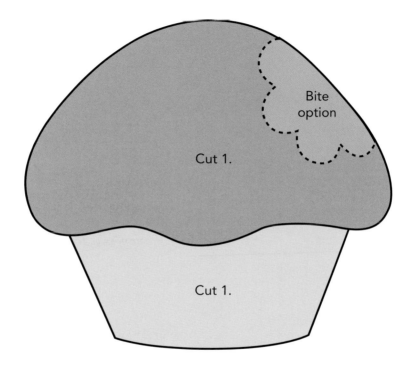

Bite
option

Cut 1.

Cut 1.

Enlarge 172% to approximately 6″ × 6″ or 229% to approximately 8″ × 8″. Cut 1 of whole cupcake.

CUPCAKE LACING TOY

contributors

Sue Astroth is an author, artist, and full-time employee of C&T Publishing. She loves to craft in the kitchen and garden when she is not playing with fabric and yarn in the studio. Sue lives in the San Francisco Bay Area.

Jane Dávila is a fiber and mixed-media artist who began her professional art career as a printmaker. She teaches art quilting and surface design workshops nationally. Jane is the co-author of *Art Quilt Workbook* and *Art Quilts at Play.* She and her husband, Carlos, an abstract oil painter, live in Ridgefield, Connecticut. You can see Jane's work at www.janedavila.com, www.janedavila.blogspot.com, and www.janedavila.etsy.com.

Fran Demar lives in the San Francisco Bay Area with her husband of 32 years and their ginger tabby cat. Sarah's Cuppy Cake Pillow is the result of quick thinking: "Mom, would you make me a cupcake quilt?" turned into a little birthday treat for a girl who has a hard time making up her mind!

Casey Dukes loves design, living simply, and making things with her hands. She lives in Northern California and is a production coordinator at C&T Publishing.

Jake Finch is a quilter, journalist, teacher, and author. She loves to create with paper, words, fabric, and pictures in new and exciting ways. Jake lives in Simi Valley, California. Visit her website at www.jakefinchdesigns.com.

Karen Flamme loves to play with fabric. She teaches art quilting and is the author of *Fast, Fun & Easy Fabric Flowers* and co-author of *Thinking Outside the Block*. Her art quilts are in galleries, juried shows, and numerous private collections. You can see more of her work at www.karenflamme.com.

Lisa Fulmer Bruce is the marketing manager at C&T Publishing. Lisa spends her spare time creating fun fiber arts and papercraft designs, several of which have been used in C&T's marketing efforts. One of her projects using a Ready-to-Go! Blank Board Book was featured in *Color Your World with Princess Mirah Batiks.* More of her work can be seen online at http://lafemmepapier.blogspot.com.

Becky Goldsmith is half of Piece O' Cake Designs—but she isn't saying whether she's the icing half or the cake! While she is known more for her appliqué quilts, she also enjoys making and collecting pincushions. Becky lives in Sherman, Texas. Visit her website at www.pieceocake.com.

Kerry Graham is a graphic designer at C&T Publishing. She enjoys making cupcakes and crafts with her children, Alivia and Hudson. Her husband, Richard, just enjoys the treats. Kerry lives in Concord, California. Visit the C&T blog at www.ctpubblog.com to see more of Kerry's craft projects.

Zinnia Heinzmann loves working with fiber, paper, and book arts and is a production coordinator at C&T Publishing. Zinnia lives in Northern California.

Lynn Koolish is a teacher, quilt book editor, and author of *Fast, Fun & Easy Fabric Dyeing* and *Fast, Fun & Easy Creative Fabric Clocks*. She works in a variety of styles and loves experimenting with new materials and techniques. Lynn lives in Berkeley, California. You can see Lynn's work at www.lynnkoolish.com.

Ruth Koolish is a long-time knitter and crocheter. She also enjoys sewing and weaving. Ruth lives in Berkeley, California.

Mary Link loves kids and crafting. A former elementary school teacher and an avid quilter, Mary enjoys combining sewing, appliqué, and soft sculpture to make useful items with an untamed flair. Mary lives in St. Paul, Minnesota.

Kiera Lofgreen is a graphic designer, artist, and craftaholic living in Northern California. You can check out more of her work at www.kieralofgreen.com/portfolio or at her Etsy store www.ProofOfConcept.etsy.com.

Gladys Love's art is an antidote to the demands of her day job as an administrative assistant at a high school, and a way to express her love of creating with textiles. She lives on Vancouver Island in British Columbia, Canada.

Joni Pike's passion for over 30 years has been sewing. A dedicated button and fabric collector, Joni designs her own line of patterns and has appeared on HGTV's Simply Quilts. Joni lives in Aurora, Colorado. Visit her website at www.sewspecialdesigns.com.

Teresa Stroin is a technical editor at C&T Publishing. She lives in Northern California with her husband, two daughters, two dogs, and a cat. Although her first love is traditional quilts, she's found that slipping a cupcake in every now and then can be fun!

Laura Wasilowski is an art quilter, surface designer, teacher, author, and dye shop owner. She combines colorful hand-dyed fabrics with personal stories to make whimsical wall pieces that often chronicle her life. Laura lives in Elgin, Illinois. Visit her website at www.artfabrik.com.

Thanks to the following for sharing their delicious recipes: Liz Aneloski, Sandy Bonsib, Lynn Koolish, Demetrice Patterson, Mary Stori, and Mary Wruck.

Special thanks to RJR Fabrics and Robert Kaufman Fabrics for providing cupcake fabric.

If you love cupcakes as much as we do, let us know at www.ctpubblog.com—search for cupcakes and add your comments. Share your cupcake stories, projects, recipes, decorating ideas...anything cupcake.

For a list of other fine books from C&T Publishing, ask for a free catalog:

C&T PUBLISHING, INC.
P.O. Box 1456
Lafayette, CA 94549
(800) 284-1114

Email: ctinfo@ctpub.com
Website: www.ctpub.com

C&T Publishing's professional photography services are now available to the public. Visit us at www.ctmediaservices.com.

For quilting supplies:

COTTON PATCH
1025 Brown Ave.
Lafayette, CA 94549
Store: (925) 284-1177
Mail order: (925) 283-7883

Email: CottonPa@aol.com
Website: www.quiltusa.com

Note: Fabrics used in the projects shown may not be currently available, as fabric manufacturers keep most fabrics in print for only a short time.